101

W R A P S

& M O R E

A Collection of Your Favorites

PUBLICATIONS INTERNATIONAL, LTD.

Front cover photography by Sanders Studios, Inc.

Pictured on the front cover: Fajitas *(page 174)*.

Pictured on the back cover *(from left to right)*: Miami Rice and Bean Burritos *(page 114)* and Stir-Fry Pita Sandwiches *(page 146)*.

ISBN: 0-7853-2475-5

Library of Congress Catalog Card Number: 98-65616

Manufactured in U.S.A.

8 7 6 5 4 3 2 1

Nutritional Analysis: The nutritional information that appears with some recipes was submitted in part by the participating companies and associations. Every effort has been made to check the accuracy of these numbers. However, because numerous variables account for a wide range of values for certain foods, nutritive analyses in this book should be considered approximate.

Microwave Cooking: Microwave ovens vary in wattage. Use the cooking times as guidelines and check for doneness before adding more time.

101

W R A P S

& M O R E

A Collection of Your Favorites

Essential WRAP FACTS

That's A Wrap!

Wraps have become one of the most popular ways to liven up everyday meals and give them an international flair. Best of all, it's fast, easy and inexpensive to wrap up a traditional Mexican burrito, an Italian sausage-stuffed calzone or a savory Mediterranean-style pita.

Not only are wraps wonderful for family meals, but they're also great for entertaining. We've included tantalizing appetizer and brunch ideas and mouthwatering main-dish recipes that will leave your guests asking for more. You'll also discover dozens of updated sandwiches that fit easily into your family's busy mealtime schedules. With *101 Wraps & More*, cooks will discover that wrapping it up adds a delicious new twist to any menu.

Around the World

Wraps are a part of many ethnic cuisines, often found as foods served by street vendors. They are the inspiration for the wraps found in restaurants and on dinner tables all across America. Not only does *101 Wraps & More* offer recipes for traditional ethnic wraps, such as tacos, enchiladas, egg rolls and gyros, but also for trendy versions.

Mexico

The tortilla, a thin unleavened flatbread, has been Mexico's everyday bread for centuries. Corn tortillas made from corn flour, or *masa*, are used for tacos and enchiladas. Flour tortillas made from wheat flour are the basis for burritos and quesadillas. Both types of tortillas are readily available in most American supermarkets.

Greece and the Middle East

Pita bread or pocket bread is popular throughout the Middle East and Greece. It is a round flatbread that can be cut in half and stuffed with a multitude of ingredients. Pita bread can also be wrapped around a filling of lamb to make a popular Greek treat known as a gyro. Pita breads made from white or whole wheat flour are available in many supermarkets.

Italy

If you like pizza, you'll love calzones. This specialty of Naples consists of a pizzalike dough wrapped around a filling; it resembles a large turnover. For a delicious Italian meal, enclose your favorite pizza toppings, cheeses and sauce in dough and bake. Or, add a new dimension to classic lasagna by spreading filling ingredients onto lasagna noodles, then rolling them up into lasagna roll-ups—what an easy update!

Asia

In China, egg roll wrappers, rice paper wrappers and moo shu pancakes are wrapped around savory fillings for spring rolls, pot stickers and moo shu. Egg roll wrappers are available in many large supermarkets and rice paper wrappers can be found in Asian markets. Moo shu pancakes are easily made at home, but flour tortillas can be substituted for a quicker version. Fillings wrapped in lettuce leaves are common in Vietnam and Thailand.

Tortilla Tips

Tortillas are best for wrapping when they are soft and flexible. When purchasing, check the sell-by date on the package. Avoid tortillas that are dry, flaky or stiff. Keep open packages tightly sealed or remove tortillas from their original packaging and wrap them tightly in plastic wrap. Store open packages of tortillas in the refrigerator for up to 10 days. Or, freeze them tightly wrapped for up to two months.

Tortillas are easier to handle and wrap when they're warm and soft. Follow any of these methods for perfectly warmed tortillas. Do not overheat tortillas or they will dry out and be difficult to wrap.

Conventional oven: Stack tortillas and wrap them in foil. Heat in a preheated 350°F oven for 10 minutes or until they are soft and hot.

Microwave oven: Stack tortillas and wrap them in plastic wrap. Microwave two tortillas on HIGH for 15 seconds. Microwave four tortillas on HIGH for 30 seconds or eight tortillas for 1 minute, turning them halfway through heating.

Grill: Stack tortillas and wrap in foil. Grill at the edge of the coals for 5 minutes, turning once until they are soft and hot. Or, grill them unwrapped over medium coals 5 to 10 seconds per side just until they are soft.

Skillet: Place flour tortillas one at a time in a nonstick skillet over medium heat. Heat about 10 seconds per side or until they are soft and hot. Corn tortillas can be lightly sprayed with water or dipped in water before heating in a nonstick skillet for 10 to 15 seconds per side.

Pita Bread Tips

Like tortillas, pita bread is best for wrapping when it is fresh. When purchasing, check the sell-by date and avoid pitas that appear dry or stiff. Leftover pita breads should be tightly sealed in their original packaging or tightly wrapped in plastic wrap. Store them at room temperature for up to two days or freeze them, tightly wrapped in foil or plastic wrap, for up to two months.

Follow either of these methods to warm pita breads for wrapping. Avoid overheating, especially on the grill because they will be difficult to wrap.

Microwave oven: Wrap one or two pita breads loosely in paper towels. Microwave on HIGH for 20 to 30 seconds or just until warm.

Grill: Place pita breads on the grill at the edge of the coals and grill them just until they are soft, about 1 to 2 minutes turning them once.

Classy
APPETIZERS & SNACKS

Chicken & Vegetable Roll-Ups

4 ounces light cream cheese, softened
2 tablespoons mayonnaise
1 tablespoon Dijon mustard (optional)
¼ teaspoon black pepper
3 (10- to 12-inch) flour tortillas
1 cup finely chopped cooked chicken
¾ cup shredded or finely chopped carrot
¾ cup finely chopped green bell pepper
3 tablespoons chopped green onion

COMBINE cream cheese, mayonnaise, mustard and black pepper in small bowl; stir until well blended.

SPREAD cream cheese mixture evenly onto each tortilla leaving ½-inch border. Divide chicken, carrot, bell pepper and onion evenly over cream cheese leaving 1½-inch border on cream cheese mixture at one end of each tortilla.

ROLL up each tortilla jelly-roll fashion. Cut each roll into 1½-inch-thick slices.

Makes 5 to 6 appetizer servings

Note: For easier slicing and to allow flavors to blend, wrap rolls in plastic wrap and refrigerate for several hours.

Chicken & Vegetable Roll-Ups

Beefy Tortilla Rolls

¼ cup GREY POUPON® COUNTRY
    DIJON® Mustard
3 ounces cream cheese, softened
2 teaspoons prepared horseradish
2 teaspoons chopped cilantro or parsley
2 (10-inch) flour tortillas
1 cup torn spinach leaves
6 ounces thinly sliced deli roast beef
1 large tomato, cut into 8 thin slices
    Lettuce leaves

In small bowl, combine mustard, cream cheese, horseradish and cilantro. Spread each tortilla with half the mustard mixture. Top each with half the spinach leaves, roast beef and tomato slices. Roll up each tortilla jelly-roll fashion. Wrap each roll in plastic wrap and chill at least 1 hour.*

To serve, cut each roll into 10 slices; arrange on lettuce-lined platter.   *Makes 20 appetizers*

*Tortilla rolls may be frozen. To serve, thaw at room temperature for 1 hour before slicing.

Chile 'n' Cheese Spirals

4 ounces cream cheese, softened
1 cup (4 ounces) shredded Cheddar cheese
½ cup (4-ounce can) ORTEGA® Diced
    Green Chiles
½ cup (about 6) sliced green onions
½ cup chopped ripe olives
4 soft taco-size (8-inch) flour tortillas
    ORTEGA® Garden Style Salsa, medium
    or mild

COMBINE cream cheese, Cheddar cheese, chiles, green onions and olives in medium bowl.

SPREAD ½ cup cheese mixture on each tortilla. Roll up. Wrap each roll in plastic wrap; chill for 1 hour.

REMOVE plastic wrap; slice each roll into six ¾-inch pieces. Serve with salsa for dipping.
          Makes 24 appetizers

Tip: Chili 'n' Cheese Spirals can be made ahead and kept in the refrigerator for 1 to 2 days. For added variety, add diced red bell pepper or use whole green chiles instead of diced.

Beefy Tortilla Rolls

Vietnamese Summer Rolls

Vietnamese Dipping Sauce (recipe
follows)
8 ounces raw medium shrimp, peeled and
deveined
3½ ounces very thin dry rice vermicelli
12 rice paper wrappers* (6½ inches in
diameter)
36 whole cilantro leaves
4 ounces roasted pork or beef, sliced ⅛ inch
thick
1 tablespoon chopped peanuts
Lime peel for garnish

*Available at specialty stores or Asian markets

1. Prepare Vietnamese Dipping Sauce; set aside.

2. Fill large saucepan ¾ full of water; bring to a
boil over high heat. Add shrimp; simmer 1 to 2
minutes or until shrimp turn pink and opaque.
Remove shrimp with slotted spoon; transfer to
small bowl.

3. Add rice vermicelli to saucepan. Cook
according to package directions until tender but
still firm, about 3 minutes. Drain in colander and
rinse under cold running water to stop cooking;
drain again.

4. Slice shrimp in half lengthwise with utility
knife.

5. To form summer rolls, soften 1 rice paper
wrapper in large bowl of water 30 to 40 seconds.
Drain and place wrapper flat on cutting board.

6. Arrange 3 cilantro leaves upside down in
center of wrapper.

7. Layer 2 shrimp halves, flat side up, over
cilantro leaves. Place layer of pork on top of
shrimp. Place ¼ cup cooked rice vermicelli over
pork.

8. To form summer rolls, fold bottom of wrapper
up over filling; fold in each side. Roll up toward
top of wrapper. Place on platter with leaf design
on top. Repeat with remaining wrappers and
fillings.

9. Sprinkle summer rolls with peanuts. Serve
with Vietnamese Dipping Sauce. Garnish, if
desired.   *Makes 12 summer rolls*

Vietnamese Dipping Sauce

½ cup water
¼ cup fish sauce
2 tablespoons lime juice
1 tablespoon sugar
1 clove garlic, minced
¼ teaspoon chili oil

Combine all ingredients in small bowl; mix well.
Makes about 1 cup

Vietnamese Summer Rolls

Roasted Garlic & Spinach Spirals

1 whole head fresh garlic
3 cups fresh spinach leaves
1 can (15 ounces) white beans, rinsed and drained
1 teaspoon dried oregano leaves
¼ teaspoon ground black pepper
⅛ teaspoon cayenne pepper
7 (7-inch) flour tortillas

1. Preheat oven to 400°F. Trim tips of garlic cloves; discard tips. Moisten head of garlic with water; wrap in foil. Bake 45 minutes or until garlic is soft and has a mellow garlicky aroma; cool. Remove garlic from skin by squeezing between fingers and thumb and place in food processor; discard stems.

2. Rinse spinach leaves; pat dry with paper towels. Remove stems; discard. Finely shred leaves by stacking and cutting several leaves at a time. Place in medium bowl.

3. Add beans, oregano, black pepper and cayenne pepper to food processor; process until smooth. Add to spinach; mix well. Spread mixture evenly onto tortillas; roll up. Trim ½ inch off ends of rolls; discard. Cut rolls into 1-inch pieces. Transfer to serving plates; garnish, if desired. *Makes 10 servings*

Note: For best results, cover tortilla rolls and refrigerate 1 to 2 hours before slicing.

Tortilla Pinwheels

1 package (8 ounces) cream cheese, softened
2 teaspoons milk
⅛ teaspoon garlic powder
1 can (4 ounces) diced green chilies, drained
1 tablespoon minced onion
  Dash of salt
8 (8- to 10-inch) flour tortillas
4 ounces very thinly sliced deli roast beef
4 ounces very thinly sliced deli roast turkey
1 can (2¼ ounces) sliced pitted black olives, drained
3 tablespoons cilantro leaves

Beat cream cheese, milk and garlic powder in medium bowl until smooth. Stir in chilies, onion and salt. Lightly moisten both sides of each tortilla with water. Spread 2 heaping tablespoons cream cheese mixture over each tortilla. Layer roast beef evenly over half of tortillas; layer turkey over remaining tortillas. Sprinkle with equal amounts of olives and cilantro. Roll up tortillas; wrap in plastic wrap. Refrigerate 1 hour or up to 8 hours. To serve, trim ½ inch from each end; discard. Cut each tortilla into six slices.
Makes 4 dozen appetizers

Roasted Garlic & Spinach Spirals

Baked Egg Rolls

Sesame Dipping Sauce (recipe follows)
1 ounce dried shiitake mushrooms
1 large carrot, shredded
1 can (8 ounces) sliced water chestnuts, drained and minced
3 green onions, minced
3 tablespoons minced fresh cilantro
12 ounces ground chicken
6 cloves garlic, minced
2 tablespoons minced fresh ginger
2 tablespoons reduced-sodium soy sauce
1 teaspoon cornstarch
2 teaspoons water
12 egg roll wrappers
1 tablespoon vegetable oil
1 teaspoon sesame seeds

1. Prepare Sesame Dipping Sauce.

2. Place mushrooms in small bowl. Cover with warm water; let stand 30 minutes or until tender. Rinse well and drain, squeezing out excess water. Cut off and discard stems. Finely chop caps; combine with carrot, water chestnuts, green onions and cilantro in large bowl.

3. Spray medium nonstick skillet with cooking spray; heat over high heat. Add chicken; cook and stir 2 minutes or until no longer pink. Add garlic and ginger; cook and stir 2 minutes more. Add to mushroom mixture. Sprinkle with soy sauce; mix well.

4. Preheat oven to 425°F. Spray baking sheet with cooking spray; set aside. Blend cornstarch and water in small bowl. Lay 1 egg roll wrapper on work surface. Spread about ⅓ cup filling

across center of wrapper to within about ½ inch of sides. Fold bottom of wrapper over filling. Fold sides in. Brush ½-inch strip across top edge with cornstarch mixture, then roll up and seal. Place seam side down on baking sheet. Repeat with remaining wrappers.

5. Brush egg rolls with oil. Sprinkle with sesame seeds. Bake 18 minutes or until golden and crisp. Serve with dipping sauce.   *Makes 12 egg rolls*

Sesame Dipping Sauce

¼ cup rice vinegar
2 teaspoons reduced-sodium soy sauce
1 teaspoon minced fresh ginger
1 teaspoon dark sesame oil

Combine all ingredients in small bowl; mix well.
Makes 5 tablespoons

Mexican Egg Rolls

2 cups (about 2 boneless, skinless breasts) finely shredded cooked chicken
2 cups (8 ounces) shredded Monterey Jack cheese
1¾ cups (16-ounce jar) ORTEGA® Garden Style Salsa, medium or mild, divided
¼ cup ORTEGA® Diced Green Chiles
10 to 12 egg roll wrappers
Vegetable oil
Sour cream (optional)

COMBINE chicken, cheese, 1 cup salsa and chiles in large bowl. Scoop ⅓ cup filling down center of each egg roll wrapper. Fold one corner over filling; fold in 2 side corners. Moisten edges of remaining corner with water; roll up egg roll from bottom. Press to seal edges. Repeat with remaining filling and wrappers.

ADD oil to 1-inch depth in medium skillet; heat over high heat for 1 minute. Place egg rolls in oil; fry, turning frequently with tongs for 1 to 2 minutes, until golden brown. Remove from skillet; place on paper towels. Serve with remaining ¾ cup salsa and sour cream.

Makes 6 servings

Taco Bread

> **1 pound (16 ounces) frozen bread dough, thawed**
> **1½ cups (6 ounces) grated cheddar cheese**
> **1 package (1.0 ounce) LAWRY'S® Taco Spices & Seasonings**
> **3 tablespoons IMPERIAL® Margarine, melted**

On baking sheet, stretch dough into 14×8-inch rectangle. Sprinkle with cheese and Taco Spices & Seasonings; drizzle with margarine. Roll up, jelly-roll fashion, and place seam-side down on baking sheet. Bake in 350°F oven 20 to 25 minutes or until golden brown. Cool.

Makes 6 servings

Spiral Reuben Dijon Bites

> **1 sheet puff pastry (½ package)**
> **¼ cup GREY POUPON® Dijon Mustard**
> **6 slices Swiss cheese (3 ounces)**
> **6 slices deli corned beef (6 ounces)**
> **1 egg, beaten**
> **1 tablespoon caraway seed**
> **Additional GREY POUPON® Dijon Mustard**

Thaw puff pastry sheet according to package directions. Roll puff pastry dough to 12×10-inch rectangle. Spread mustard evenly over dough; top with cheese and corned beef. Cut in half crosswise to form 2 (10×6-inch) rectangles. Roll up each rectangle from short end, jelly-roll fashion; pinch seams to seal.*

Cut each roll into 16 (¼-inch-thick) slices. Place slices, cut sides up, on lightly greased baking sheets; brush with beaten egg and sprinkle with caraway seed. Bake at 400°F for 10 to 12 minutes or until golden. Serve warm with additional mustard.

Makes 32 appetizers

*Rolls may be wrapped and frozen. To serve, thaw at room temperature for 30 minutes. Slice and bake as directed above.

Roasted Eggplant Rolls

2 medium eggplants (¾ pound each)
2 tablespoons lemon juice
1 teaspoon olive oil
4 tablespoons (2 ounces) fat-free cream
   cheese
2 tablespoons nonfat sour cream
1 green onion, minced
4 sun-dried tomatoes (packed in oil),
   drained and minced
1 clove garlic, minced
¼ teaspoon dried oregano leaves
⅛ teaspoon black pepper
16 medium spinach leaves, washed, stemmed
   and dried
1 cup bottled spaghetti sauce

1. Preheat oven to 450°F. Spray 2 nonstick baking sheets with nonstick cooking spray; set aside. Trim ends from eggplants; cut lengthwise into ¼-inch-thick slices. Discard outside slices that are mostly skin. (You will have about 16 slices.)

2. Combine lemon juice and olive oil in small bowl; brush lightly over both sides of eggplant slices. Arrange slices in single layer on baking sheets. Bake 10 to 12 minutes or until slightly golden brown on bottom. Turn slices over and bake 10 to 12 minutes more or until golden on both sides and tender. (Slices may not brown evenly; turn slices as they brown. Some very dark spots will occur.) Transfer slices to plate; cool.

3. Meanwhile, stir cream cheese in small bowl until smooth. Add sour cream, green onion, tomatoes, garlic, oregano and pepper; stir until blended.

4. Place eggplant slices on work surface; spread about 2 teaspoons cream cheese mixture evenly over each slice. Arrange spinach leaves on top leaving ½-inch border. Roll up, beginning at narrower end; lay rolls seam sides down on serving platter. (If making ahead, cover and refrigerate up to 2 days. Bring to room temperature before serving.) Serve with warm spaghetti sauce.   *Makes 8 servings (2 rolls each)*

Mexican Roll-Ups

6 uncooked lasagna noodles
¾ cup prepared guacamole
¾ cup chunky salsa
¾ cup (3 ounces) shredded nonfat Cheddar
   cheese
Additional salsa (optional)

Cook lasagna noodles according to package directions. Rinse with cold water; drain. Cool. Spread 2 tablespoons guacamole and 2 tablespoons salsa over each noodle; sprinkle each with 2 tablespoons cheese. Roll up noodles jelly-roll fashion. Cut each roll-up in half to form two equal-size roll-ups. Serve immediately with salsa or cover with plastic wrap and refrigerate up to 3 hours.   *Makes 12 appetizers*

Roasted Eggplant Rolls

Turkey-Broccoli Roll-Ups

    2 pounds broccoli
    ⅓ cup nonfat sour cream
    ¼ cup reduced-calorie mayonnaise
    2 tablespoons thawed frozen orange juice
        concentrate
    1 tablespoon Dijon mustard
    1 teaspoon dried basil leaves, crushed
    1 pound smoked turkey, very thinly sliced

1. Trim large leaves and tough ends of lower stalks from broccoli; discard. Wash broccoli. Cut stalks lengthwise, including flowerets, to form approximately 40 (3-inch) spears.

2. Arrange broccoli spears in single layer in large, shallow microwavable dish. Add 1 tablespoon water. Cover dish tightly with heavy-duty plastic wrap; vent. Microwave at HIGH 6 to 7 minutes or just until broccoli is crisp-tender, rearranging spears after 4 minutes. Carefully remove plastic wrap; drain broccoli. Immediately place broccoli in cold water to prevent additional cooking; drain well. Pat dry with paper towels.

3. Combine sour cream, mayonnaise, orange juice concentrate, mustard and basil in small bowl; mix well.

4. Cut turkey slices into 2-inch-wide strips. Spread sour cream mixture evenly onto strips. Place 1 broccoli piece at short end of each strip. Starting at short end, roll up tightly (allow broccoli floweret to protrude from one end). Place on serving platter; cover with plastic wrap. Refrigerate until ready to serve. Garnish just before serving, if desired.   *Makes 20 servings*

Note: To blanch broccoli on stove top, bring small amount of water to a boil in saucepan. Add broccoli spears; cover. Simmer 2 to 3 minutes or until broccoli is crisp-tender; drain. Cool; continue as directed.

Black Bean Tortilla Pinwheels

    1 (8-ounce) package cream cheese, softened
    1 cup dairy sour cream
    1 cup (4 ounces) shredded Wisconsin
        Monterey Jack cheese
    ¼ cup chopped, well-drained pimento-stuffed
        green olives
    ¼ cup chopped red onion
    ½ teaspoon seasoned salt
    ⅛ teaspoon garlic powder
    1 (15-ounce) can black beans, drained
    5 (10-inch) flour tortillas
    Salsa

Beat cream cheese and sour cream in medium bowl until well blended. Stir in Monterey Jack cheese, olives, onion, salt and garlic powder. Cover; refrigerate 2 hours. Place beans in food processor or blender; process until smooth. Spread each tortilla with thin layer of beans. Spread thin layer of cream cheese mixture over beans. Roll up tortillas tightly. Wrap in plastic wrap; refrigerate until chilled. Cut tortillas into ¾-inch slices. Serve with salsa. Garnish as desired.   *Makes 12 to 16 appetizer servings*

Favorite recipe from **Wisconsin Milk Marketing Board**

Sausage Pinwheels

2 cups biscuit mix
½ cup milk
¼ cup butter or margarine, melted
1 pound BOB EVANS® Original Recipe
　　Roll Sausage

Combine biscuit mix, milk and butter in large bowl until blended. Refrigerate 30 minutes. Divide dough into two portions. Roll out one portion on floured surface to ⅛-inch-thick rectangle, about 10×7 inches. Spread with half the sausage. Roll lengthwise into long roll. Repeat with remaining dough and sausage. Place rolls in freezer until hard enough to cut easily. Preheat oven to 400°F. Cut rolls into thin slices. Place on baking sheets. Bake 15 minutes or until golden brown. Serve hot. Refrigerate leftovers.

Makes 48 appetizers

Note: This recipe may be doubled. Refreeze after slicing. When ready to serve, thaw slices in refrigerator and bake.

Piña Quesadillas

1 can (8 ounces) DOLE® Crushed
　　Pineapple, well drained
1 small tomato, chopped
2 tablespoons finely chopped DOLE® Green
　　Onion
2 tablespoons chopped jalapeño chilies
1 cup (4 ounces) shredded Monterey Jack
　　cheese
4 (8-inch) flour tortillas
　　Vegetable cooking spray
　　Sour cream (optional)

• Combine drained pineapple, tomato, green onion and chilies in small bowl.

• Sprinkle pineapple mixture and cheese evenly over one half of each tortilla. Fold each tortilla in half to form quesadillas, lightly pressing down.

• Place 2 quesadillas in large skillet sprayed with vegetable cooking spray. Cook over medium heat 3 to 5 minutes or until cheese melts, turning once halfway through cooking. Remove from skillet and repeat with remaining 2 quesadillas.

• Cut each quesadilla into 3 triangles. Serve with sour cream, if desired.　　*Makes 4 servings*

Prep Time: 15 minutes
Cook Time: 5 minutes

Bean and Vegetable Egg Rolls

   Plum Dipping Sauce (recipe follows)
1 tablespoon sesame seeds
1 tablespoon Oriental sesame oil
2 green onions with tops, sliced
1 tablespoon minced fresh ginger
2 cloves garlic, minced
2 cups shredded napa cabbage
1 cup shredded carrots
½ cup chopped celery
½ cup chopped mushrooms
4 ounces fresh or canned bean sprouts,
   rinsed and drained
1 can (15 ounces) chick-peas, rinsed and
   drained
1½ teaspoons reduced-sodium soy sauce
   Pepper (optional)
1 egg, beaten
12 egg roll wrappers
   Peanut or vegetable oil

1. Prepare Plum Dipping Sauce.

2. Combine sesame seeds and sesame oil in large skillet. Cook and stir over low heat 2 to 3 minutes or until sesame seeds begin to brown. Add green onions, ginger and garlic; cook and stir 1 to 2 minutes. Add cabbage, carrots, celery, mushrooms and bean sprouts; cover. Cook 8 minutes or until cabbage is wilted. Stir in chick-peas and soy sauce; season to taste with pepper, if desired. Cool 10 minutes; stir in egg.

3. Place ⅓ cup vegetable mixture near one corner of egg roll wrapper. Brush edges of egg roll wrapper with water. Fold bottom corner of egg roll wrapper up over filling; fold sides in and roll up. Repeat with remaining filling and egg roll wrappers.

4. Heat 1 inch peanut oil in large, heavy saucepan over medium-high heat until oil is 375°F; adjust heat to maintain temperature. Fry egg rolls 3 to 5 minutes or until golden. Drain on paper towels; serve hot with Plum Dipping Sauce. Garnish, if desired.   *Makes 12 servings*

Plum Dipping Sauce

⅔ cup plum sauce
3 tablespoons reduced-sodium soy sauce
2 tablespoons rice vinegar or cider vinegar
1 tablespoon grated fresh ginger
1 tablespoon honey
2 green onions with tops, sliced
3 to 4 drops hot chili oil (optional)

1. Combine all ingredients in medium bowl; mix well. Cover; refrigerate until ready to serve.
                              Makes about 1 cup

Bean and Vegetable Egg Roll

Savory Sausage Mushroom Turnovers

1 (12-ounce) package frozen bulk pork
    sausage, thawed
1 cup chopped mushrooms
⅓ cup chopped onion
½ cup shredded Swiss cheese (2 ounces)
⅓ cup GREY POUPON® COUNTRY
    DIJON® Mustard
2 tablespoons diced red bell pepper
½ teaspoon dried thyme leaves
2 (8-ounce) packages refrigerated crescent
    dinner roll dough
1 egg, beaten
    Sesame or poppy seed

In large skillet, over medium heat, cook sausage, mushrooms and onion until sausage is cooked, stirring occasionally to break up sausage. Remove from heat. Stir in cheese, mustard, bell pepper and thyme.

Separate each package of dough into 4 rectangles; press perforations together to seal. On floured surface, roll each rectangle into 6-inch square. Cut each square into quarters, making 32 squares total. Place 1 scant tablespoon sausage mixture on each square; fold dough over filling on the diagonal to form triangle. Press edges with fork to seal. Place on greased baking sheets.

Brush triangles with beaten egg and sprinkle with sesame or poppy seed. Bake at 375°F for 10 to 12 minutes or until golden brown. Serve warm.

Makes 32 appetizers

Spinach Cheese Triangles

1 package (8 ounces) PHILADELPHIA
    BRAND® Cream Cheese, softened
1 package (10 ounces) frozen chopped
    spinach, thawed, well drained
⅓ cup chopped drained roasted red peppers
¼ teaspoon garlic salt
6 sheets frozen phyllo, thawed
½ cup (1 stick) butter or margarine, melted

MIX cream cheese, spinach, red peppers and garlic salt with electric mixer on medium speed until well blended.

LAY 1 phyllo sheet on flat surface. Brush with some of the melted butter. Cut lengthwise into 4 (18×3½-inch) strips.

SPOON about 1 tablespoon filling about 1 inch from one end of each strip. Fold the end over the filling at a 45-degree angle. Continue folding as you would fold a flag to form a triangle that encloses filling. Repeat procedure with remaining phyllo sheets. Place triangles on cookie sheet. Brush with melted butter.

BAKE at 375°F for 12 to 15 minutes or until golden brown. *Makes 3 dozen*

Tip: Unfold phyllo sheets; cover with wax paper and damp kitchen towel to prevent drying until ready to use.

Prep Time: 30 minutes
Baking Time: 15 minutes

*Savory Sausage Mushroom
Turnovers*

Gingered Chicken Pot Stickers

3 cups finely shredded cabbage
1 egg white, lightly beaten
1 tablespoon light soy sauce
¼ teaspoon crushed red pepper
1 tablespoon minced fresh ginger
4 green onions with tops, finely chopped
¼ pound ground chicken breast, cooked and drained
24 wonton wrappers, at room temperature
    Cornstarch
½ cup water
1 tablespoon oyster sauce
½ teaspoon honey
⅛ teaspoon crushed red pepper
2 teaspoons grated lemon peel
1 tablespoon peanut oil

Steam cabbage 5 minutes, then cool to room temperature. Squeeze out any excess moisture; set aside. To prepare filling, combine egg white, soy sauce, ¼ teaspoon red pepper, ginger and green onions in large bowl; blend well. Stir in cabbage and chicken.

To prepare pot stickers, place 1 tablespoon filling in center of 1 wonton wrapper. Gather edges around filling, pressing firmly at top to seal. Repeat with remaining wrappers and filling. Place pot stickers on large baking sheet dusted with cornstarch. Refrigerate 1 hour or until cold. Meanwhile, to prepare sauce, combine remaining ingredients except oil in small bowl; mix well. Set aside.

Heat oil in large nonstick skillet over high heat. Add pot stickers and cook until bottoms are golden brown. Pour sauce over top. Cover and cook 3 minutes. Uncover and cook until all liquid is absorbed. Serve warm on tray as finger food or on small plates with chopsticks as first course.   *Makes 8 appetizer servings*

Sesame Chicken Salad Wonton Cups

Nonstick cooking spray
20 (3-inch) wonton wrappers
1 tablespoon sesame seeds
2 small boneless skinless chicken breasts (about 8 ounces)
1 cup fresh green beans, cut diagonally into ½-inch pieces
¼ cup reduced-calorie mayonnaise
1 tablespoon chopped fresh cilantro (optional)
2 teaspoons honey
1 teaspoon reduced-sodium soy sauce
⅛ teaspoon cayenne pepper

1. Preheat oven to 350°F. Spray miniature muffin pan with nonstick cooking spray. Press 1 wonton wrapper into each muffin cup; spray with nonstick cooking spray. Bake 8 to 10 minutes or until golden brown. Cool in pan on wire rack before filling.

2. Place sesame seeds in shallow baking pan. Bake 5 minutes or until lightly toasted, stirring occasionally. Set aside to cool.

3. Meanwhile, bring 2 cups water to a boil in medium saucepan. Add chicken. Reduce heat to low; cover. Simmer 10 minutes or until chicken is no longer pink in center, adding green beans after 7 minutes. Drain.

4. Finely chop chicken. Place in medium bowl. Add green beans and remaining ingredients; mix lightly. Spoon lightly rounded tablespoonful of chicken mixture into each wonton cup. Garnish, if desired. *Makes 10 servings*

Dim Sum Baked Buns

9 (18 ounces) frozen bread dough rolls
6 to 8 dried shiitake mushrooms
3 green onions, minced
2 tablespoons plum sauce
1 tablespoon hoisin sauce
8 ounces ground chicken
4 cloves garlic, minced
1 tablespoon minced fresh ginger
2 tablespoons cholesterol-free egg substitute
¾ teaspoon sesame seeds

1. Thaw frozen rolls following package directions.

2. Place mushrooms in small bowl. Cover with warm water; let stand 30 minutes. Rinse well and drain, squeezing out excess water. Cut off and discard stems. Finely chop caps. Combine mushrooms, green onions, plum sauce and hoisin sauce in large bowl.

3. Spray medium nonstick skillet with cooking spray; heat over high heat. Add chicken; cook without stirring 1 to 2 minutes or until no longer pink. Add garlic and ginger; cook and stir 2 minutes more. Add mushroom mixture; mix well.

4. Spray 2 baking sheets with cooking spray. Lightly flour hands and work surface. Cut each roll in half; roll each piece into a ball. Shape each piece between hands to form disk. Press edge of disk between thumb and forefinger, working in circular motion to form circle 3 to 3½ inches in diameter (center of disk should be thicker than edges.)

5. Place disk flat on work surface. Place 1 generous tablespoon filling in center. Lift edges of dough up and around filling; pinch edges of dough together to seal. Place seam side down on baking sheet. Repeat with remaining dough and filling.

6. Cover buns with towel; let rise in warm place 45 minutes or until buns have doubled in size. Meanwhile, preheat oven to 375°F. Brush buns with egg, then sprinkle with sesame seeds. Bake 16 to 18 minutes or until buns are golden brown.
Makes 18 buns

Spinach-Stuffed Appetizer Shells

18 jumbo pasta shells (about 6 ounces)
1 package (10 ounces) frozen chopped
    spinach, thawed and very well drained
1 can (8 ounces) water chestnuts, drained
    and chopped
¾ cup nonfat ricotta cheese
½ cup reduced-calorie mayonnaise
¼ cup finely chopped carrot
3 tablespoons finely chopped onion
¾ teaspoon garlic powder
¾ teaspoon hot pepper sauce

1. Cook shells according to package directions,
omitting salt. Rinse under cold running water
until shells are cool; drain well.

2. Combine remaining ingredients in medium
bowl; mix well.

3. Fill each shell with approximately 3
tablespoons spinach mixture; cover. Refrigerate
up to 12 hours before serving. Garnish, if desired.
                                    Makes 18 shells

Sausage Puffed Pockets

1 (15-ounce) package prepared pie crust
    (2 crusts)
¼ pound BOB EVANS® Original Recipe
    Roll Sausage
2 tablespoons finely chopped onion
⅛ teaspoon dried oregano leaves
⅛ teaspoon garlic powder
⅛ teaspoon ground cumin
1 tablespoon chopped pimiento-stuffed
    olives
1 tablespoon chopped raisins
1 egg, separated

Let pie crusts stand at room temperature 20
minutes or according to package directions.
Meanwhile, crumble sausage into medium skillet.
Add onion, oregano, garlic powder and cumin.
Cook over medium-high heat until sausage is
browned, stirring occasionally. Drain off any
drippings. Stir in olives and raisins. Beat egg yolk
slightly; stir into sausage mixture, mixing well.
Preheat oven to 425°F. Carefully unfold crusts.
Cut into desired shapes using 3-inch cookie
cutters. Place about 2 teaspoons sausage mixture
on half the cutouts. Top with remaining dough
shapes. Moisten fingers with water and pinch
dough to seal edges. Slightly beat egg white;
gently brush over top of pockets. Bake 15 to 18
minutes or until lightly browned. Serve hot.
Refrigerate leftovers.   *Makes 12 appetizers*

Spinach-Stuffed Appetizer Shells

Onion and Pepper Calzones

    1 teaspoon vegetable oil
 ½ cup chopped onion
 ½ cup chopped green bell pepper
 ¼ teaspoon salt
 ⅛ teaspoon dried basil leaves
 ⅛ teaspoon dried oregano leaves
 ⅛ teaspoon black pepper
    1 can (12 ounces) country biscuits
        (10 biscuits)
 ¼ cup (1 ounce) shredded mozzarella cheese
 ½ cup prepared spaghetti or pizza sauce
    2 tablespoons grated Parmesan cheese

1. Preheat oven to 400°F. Heat oil in medium nonstick skillet over medium-high heat. Add onion and bell pepper. Cook and stir 5 minutes. Remove from heat. Add salt, basil, oregano and black pepper; stir to combine. Cool slightly.

2. While onion mixture is cooling, flatten biscuits into 3½-inch circles about ⅛ inch thick.

3. Stir mozzarella cheese into onion mixture; spoon 1 teaspoonful onto each biscuit. Fold biscuits in half, covering filling. Press edges with tines of fork to seal; transfer to baking sheet.

4. Bake 10 to 12 minutes or until golden brown. Meanwhile, place spaghetti sauce in small microwavable bowl. Cover with vented plastic wrap. Microwave on HIGH 3 minutes or until hot.

5. To serve, spoon spaghetti sauce over calzones. Sprinkle with Parmesan cheese.

Makes 10 appetizers

Prep and cook time: 25 minutes

Greek-Style Grilled Feta

 ¼ cup thinly sliced sweet onion
    1 package (8 ounces) feta cheese, sliced in
        half horizontally
 ¼ cup thinly sliced green bell pepper
 ¼ cup thinly sliced red bell pepper
 ½ teaspoon dried oregano leaves
 ¼ teaspoon garlic pepper or ground black
        pepper
    24 (½-inch-thick) slices French bread

1. Spray 14-inch-long sheet of foil with nonstick cooking spray. Place onion slices in center of foil and top with feta slices. Sprinkle with bell pepper slices, oregano and garlic pepper.

2. Seal foil using Drugstore Wrap technique.* Place foil packet on grid upside down and grill on covered grill over hot coals 15 minutes. Turn packet over; grill on covered grill 15 minutes more.

3. Open packet carefully and serve immediately with slices of French bread.   *Makes 8 servings*

*To ensure even cooking without any leakage, use the Drugstore Wrap technique. Place the food in the center of an oblong piece of heavy-duty foil, leaving at least a two-inch border around the food. Bring the two long sides together above the food; fold down in a series of locked folds, allowing for heat circulation and expansion. Fold the short ends up and over again. Press folds firmly to seal the foil packet.

Artichoke Crostini

1 jar (6 ounces) marinated artichoke hearts, drained and chopped
3 green onions, chopped
5 tablespoons grated Parmesan cheese, divided
2 tablespoons mayonnaise
12 slices French bread, ½ inch thick

1. Preheat broiler. Combine artichokes, green onions, 3 tablespoons cheese and mayonnaise in small bowl; mix well.

2. Arrange bread slices on baking sheet. Broil 4 to 5 inches from heat source 2 to 3 minutes onto each side or until lightly browned.

3. Remove baking sheet from broiler. Spoon about 1 tablespoon artichoke mixture on each bread slice and sprinkle with remaining 2 tablespoons cheese. Broil 1 to 2 minutes or until cheese is melted and lightly browned.

Makes 4 servings

Serve It With Style: Garnish crostini with red bell pepper, if desired.

Prep and cook time: 25 minutes

Smoked Salmon Appetizers

¼ cup reduced-fat or fat-free cream cheese, softened
1 tablespoon chopped fresh dill *or* 1 teaspoon dried dill weed
⅛ teaspoon ground red pepper
4 ounces thinly sliced smoked salmon or lox
24 melba toast rounds or other low-fat crackers

1. Combine cream cheese, dill and pepper in small bowl; stir to blend. Spread evenly over each slice of salmon. Starting with short side, roll up salmon slices jelly-roll fashion. Place on plate; cover with plastic wrap. Chill at least 1 hour or up to 4 hours before serving.

2. Using a sharp knife, cut salmon rolls crosswise into ¾-inch pieces. Place pieces, cut side down, on serving plate. Garnish each piece with dill sprig, if desired. Serve cold or at room temperature with melba rounds.

Makes about 2 dozen appetizers

Artichoke Crostini

Smoked Chicken Bagel Snacks

⅓ cup fat-free cream cheese, softened
2 teaspoons spicy brown mustard
¼ cup chopped commercial roasted red peppers, drained
1 green onion with top, sliced
5 mini-bagels, split
3 ounces smoked chicken or turkey, cut into 10 very thin slices
¼ medium cucumber, cut into 10 thin slices

1. Combine cream cheese and mustard in small bowl; mix well. Stir in peppers and green onion.

2. Spread cream cheese mixture evenly onto cut sides of bagels. Cover bottom halves of bagels with chicken, folding chicken to fit onto bagels; top with cucumber slices and tops of bagels.

Makes 5 servings

Stuffed Party Baguette

2 medium red bell peppers
1 French bread loaf, about 14 inches long
¼ cup plus 2 tablespoons fat-free Italian dressing, divided
1 small red onion, very thinly sliced
8 large fresh basil leaves
3 ounces Swiss cheese, very thinly sliced

1. Preheat oven to 425°F. Cover large baking sheet with foil.

2. To roast bell peppers, cut peppers in half; remove stems, seeds and membranes. Place peppers, cut sides down, on prepared baking sheet. Bake 20 to 25 minutes or until skins are browned, turning occasionally.

3. Transfer peppers from baking sheet to paper bag; close bag tightly. Let stand 10 minutes or until peppers are cool enough to handle and skins are loosened. Peel off skins using sharp knife; discard skins. Cut peppers into strips.

4. Trim ends from bread; discard. Cut loaf lengthwise in half. Remove soft insides of loaf; reserve removed bread for another use.

5. Brush ¼ cup Italian dressing evenly onto cut sides of bread. Arrange pepper strips in even layer in bottom half of loaf; top with even layer of onion. Brush onion with remaining 2 tablespoons Italian dressing; top with layer of basil and cheese. Replace bread top. Wrap loaf tightly in heavy-duty plastic wrap; refrigerate at least 2 hours or overnight.

6. When ready to serve, cut loaf crosswise into 1-inch slices. Secure with wooden picks and garnish, if desired.

Makes 12 servings

Smoked Chicken Bagel Snacks

Pleasing
POULTRY WRAPS

Pesto Chicken & Pepper Wraps

⅔ cup refrigerated pesto sauce or frozen pesto sauce, thawed and divided
3 tablespoons red wine vinegar
¼ teaspoon salt
¼ teaspoon black pepper
1¼ pounds skinless boneless chicken thighs or breasts
2 red bell peppers, cut in half, stemmed and seeded
5 (8-inch) flour tortillas
5 thin slices (3-inch rounds) fresh-pack mozzarella cheese*
5 leaves Boston or red leaf lettuce
Orange slices
Red and green chilies
Fresh basil sprigs

*Packaged sliced whole milk or part-skim mozzarella cheese can be substituted for fresh-pack mozzarella cheese.

Combine ¼ cup pesto, vinegar, salt and black pepper in medium bowl. Add chicken; toss to coat. Cover and refrigerate at least 30 minutes. Remove chicken from marinade; discard marinade. Grill chicken over medium-hot KINGSFORD® briquets about 4 minutes per side until chicken is no longer pink in center, turning once. Grill bell peppers, skin sides down, about 8 minutes until skin is charred. Place bell peppers in large resealable plastic food storage bag; seal. Let stand 5 minutes; remove skin. Cut chicken and bell peppers into thin strips. Spread about 1 tablespoon of remaining pesto down center of each tortilla; top with chicken, bell peppers, cheese and lettuce. Roll tortillas to enclose filling. Garnish with orange slices, chilies and basil sprigs.
Makes 5 wraps

Pesto Chicken & Pepper Wrap

Chicken Enchiladas

1¾ cups fat free sour cream
½ cup chopped green onions
⅓ cup minced fresh cilantro
1 tablespoon minced fresh jalapeño chili pepper
1 teaspoon ground cumin
1 tablespoon vegetable oil
12 ounces boneless, skinless chicken breasts, cut into 3×1-inch strips
1 teaspoon minced garlic
8 flour tortillas (8-inch)
1 cup (4 ounces) shredded ALPINE LACE® Reduced Fat Cheddar Cheese
1 cup bottled chunky salsa (medium or hot)
1 small ripe tomato, chopped
Sprigs of cilantro (optional)

1. Preheat the oven to 350°F. Spray a 13×9×3-inch baking dish with nonstick cooking spray.

2. In a small bowl, mix together the sour cream, green onions, cilantro, jalapeño pepper and cumin.

3. Spray a large nonstick skillet with the cooking spray, pour in the oil and heat over medium-high heat. Add the chicken and garlic and sauté for 4 minutes or until the juices run clear when the chicken is pierced with a fork.

4. Divide the chicken strips among the 8 tortillas, placing them down the center of the tortillas. Top with the sour cream mixture, then roll them up and place them, seam side down, in the baking dish.

5. Sprinkle with the cheese, cover with foil and bake for 30 minutes or until bubbly. Spoon the salsa in a strip down the center and sprinkle the salsa with the tomato. Garnish with sprigs of cilantro, if you wish. Serve hot!

Makes 8 servings

Red, White and Yellow Spinach Wrap

1 package (15 ounces) MAHATMA® or CAROLINA® Saffron Yellow rice
2 tablespoons vegetable oil
1 small, sliced green bell pepper
1 small, sliced red bell pepper
1 small, sliced white onion
2 skinless, boneless chicken breasts
4 large (burrito size) flour tortillas
¼ pound spinach leaves, cleaned
1 cup (4 ounces) shredded mild Cheddar cheese

Prepare rice according to package directions. While rice is cooking, heat oil in medium skillet; sauté peppers and onion. Remove from skillet; set aside. In same pan, brown chicken breasts on both sides, cooking until chicken is no longer pink. Remove from skillet and cut in thin slices.

Lay tortillas on flat surface. Line each with spinach leaves. Divide rice in four equal parts, spreading evenly over spinach. Divide vegetables, chicken and cheese among tortillas. Roll tortillas. Wrap in butcher paper or foil to serve.

Makes 4 servings

Chicken Enchiladas

Soft Turkey Tacos

8 (6-inch) corn tortillas*
1½ teaspoons vegetable oil
1 pound ground turkey
1 small onion, chopped
1 teaspoon dried oregano leaves
Salt and pepper
Chopped tomatoes
Shredded lettuce
Salsa
Refried beans (optional)

*Substitute 8 (10-inch) flour tortillas for corn tortillas, if desired.

1. Wrap tortillas in foil. Place in cold oven; set temperature to 350°F.

2. Heat oil in large skillet over medium heat. Add turkey and onion; cook until turkey is no longer pink, stirring occasionally. Stir in oregano. Season with salt and pepper to taste. Keep warm.

3. For each taco, fill warm tortilla with turkey mixture; top with tomatoes, lettuce and salsa. Serve with refried beans, if desired.

Makes 4 servings

Note: To warm tortillas in microwave oven, wrap loosely in damp paper towel. Microwave on HIGH (100%) 2 minutes or until hot.

Chicken Fajita Wraps

1 pound chicken tenders
¼ cup lime juice
4 cloves garlic, minced, divided
1 red bell pepper, sliced
1 green bell pepper, sliced
1 yellow bell pepper, sliced
1 large red onion, cut into ¼-inch slices
½ teaspoon ground cumin
¼ teaspoon salt
¼ teaspoon ground red pepper
8 (8-inch) flour tortillas, warmed
Salsa

1. Combine chicken, lime juice and 2 cloves garlic in medium bowl; toss to coat. Cover and marinate 30 minutes in refrigerator, stirring occasionally.

2. Spray large nonstick skillet with nonstick cooking spray; heat over medium heat until hot. Add chicken mixture; cook and stir 5 to 7 minutes or until chicken is browned and no longer pink in center. Remove chicken from skillet. Drain excess liquid from skillet, if necessary.

3. Add bell peppers, onion and remaining 2 cloves garlic to skillet; cook and stir about 5 minutes or until vegetables are tender. Sprinkle with cumin, salt and red pepper. Return chicken to skillet; cook and stir 1 to 2 minutes.

4. Fill tortillas with chicken mixture. Serve with salsa. Garnish, if desired. *Makes 4 servings*

Turkey & Zucchini Enchiladas with Tomatillo-Green Chile Sauce

1¼ pound turkey leg
1 tablespoon olive oil
1 small onion, thinly sliced
1 tablespoon minced garlic
1 pound zucchini, quartered lengthwise, sliced thinly crosswise
1½ teaspoons cumin
½ teaspoon dried oregano leaves crushed
¾ cup (3 ounces) shredded reduced-fat Monterey Jack cheese
12 (6-inch) corn tortillas
Tomatillo-Green Chile Sauce (recipe follows)
½ cup crumbled feta cheese

1. Place turkey in large saucepan; cover with water. Bring to a boil over high heat. Reduce heat. Cover and simmer 1½ to 2 hours or until tender. Drain; discard skin and bone. Cut meat into small pieces. Place in medium bowl.

2. Preheat oven to 350°F.

3. Heat oil over medium-high heat in large skillet. Add onion; cook and stir 3 to 4 minutes or until tender. Reduce heat to medium. Add garlic; cook and stir 3 to 4 minutes or until onion is golden. Add zucchini, 2 tablespoons water, cumin and oregano. Cover; cook over medium heat 10 minutes until zucchini is soft. Add to turkey. Stir in Monterey Jack cheese.

4. Heat large nonstick skillet over medium-high heat. Place 1 inch water in medium bowl. Dip 1 tortilla in water; shake off excess. Place in hot skillet. Cook 10 to 15 seconds on each side or until tortilla is hot and pliable. Repeat with remaining tortillas.

5. Spray bottom of 13×9-inch baking pan with nonstick cooking spray. Spoon ¼ cup filling in center of each tortilla; fold sides over to enclose. Place seam side down in pan. Brush tops with ½ cup Tomatillo-Green Chile Sauce. Cover; bake 30 to 40 minutes or until hot. Top enchiladas with remaining Tomatillo-Green Chile Sauce and feta cheese. *Makes 6 servings*

Tomatillo-Green Chile Sauce

2 cans (18 ounces each) whole tomatillos, drained
1 can (4 ounces) diced mild green chilies, drained
½ teaspoon ground cumin
1 teaspoon dried oregano leaves, crushed
2 tablespoons chopped fresh cilantro

1. Place tomatillos, chilies, cumin and oregano in food processor or blender; process until smooth. Place in large saucepan. Cover; heat over medium heat until bubbling. Stir in cilantro. *Makes about 3 cups*

Spicy Lime and Cilantro Turkey Fajitas

     1 pound Turkey Tenderloins
     1 tablespoon paprika
     ½ teaspoon onion salt
     ½ teaspoon garlic powder
     ½ teaspoon ground red pepper
     ½ teaspoon fennel seeds
     ½ teaspoon dried thyme leaves
     ¼ teaspoon white pepper
        Sour Cream Sauce (recipe follows)
     1 lime, halved
     4 pita breads
        Shredded lettuce (optional)

1. Slice tenderloins open lengthwise, cutting almost through, being careful to leave halves attached. Open halves flat. In shallow flat dish, combine paprika, onion salt, garlic powder, red pepper, fennel, thyme and white pepper. Rub mixture over tenderloins; cover and refrigerate 1 hour. Prepare Sour Cream Sauce.

2. Prepare grill for direct cooking. Grill tenderloins, on covered grill, 10 to 12 minutes or until meat thermometer inserted into thickest part of tenderloin registers 170°F, turning halfway through grilling time. Place on clean serving plate; squeeze lime over tenderloins. Cut tenderloins crosswise into ¼-inch-thick slices.

3. To serve, top each pita with tenderloins and Sour Cream Sauce; roll up. Garnish with lettuce, if desired. *Makes 4 servings*

Sour Cream Sauce

     1 cup fat-free sour cream
     ¼ cup thinly sliced green onions
     ¼ cup finely chopped cilantro
     1 can (4 ounces) green chilies, drained
     1 plum tomato, seeded and finely chopped
     ½ teaspoon black pepper
     ¼ teaspoon ground red pepper

In small bowl, combine sour cream, green onions, cilantro, chilies, tomato, black and ground red peppers. Cover; refrigerate until ready to use.

Favorite recipe from **National Turkey Federation**

Chicken and Vegetable Tortilla Roll-Ups

1 pound boneless skinless chicken breasts, cooked
1 cup chopped broccoli
1 cup diced carrots
1 can (10¾ ounces) condensed cream of celery soup
¼ cup 2% milk
1 tablespoon dry sherry
½ cup grated Parmesan cheese
6 (10-inch) flour tortillas

PREHEAT oven to 350°F. Cut chicken into 1-inch pieces; set aside.

COMBINE broccoli and carrots in 1-quart microwavable dish. Cover and microwave at HIGH 2 to 3 minutes or until vegetables are crisp-tender; set aside.

COMBINE soup, milk and sherry in small saucepan over medium heat; cook and stir 5 minutes. Stir in Parmesan cheese, chicken, broccoli and carrots; season to taste with salt and pepper. Cook 2 minutes or until cheese is melted. Remove from heat.

SPOON ¼ cup chicken mixture onto each tortilla. Roll up and place seam side down in 13×9-inch baking dish coated with nonstick cooking spray. Bake covered 20 minutes or until heated through.   *Makes 6 servings*

Turkey Ham Quesadillas

¼ cup picante sauce or salsa
4 (7-inch) regular or whole wheat flour tortillas
½ cup shredded reduced-sodium reduced-fat Monterey Jack cheese
¼ cup finely chopped turkey ham or lean ham
¼ cup canned green chilies, drained *or* 1 to 2 tablespoons chopped fresh jalapeño* to taste
Nonstick cooking spray
Additional picante sauce or salsa for dipping (optional)
Fat-free or low-fat sour cream (optional)

*Jalapeño peppers can sting and irritate the skin; wear rubber gloves when handling and do not touch eyes. Wash hands after handling.

1. Spread 1 tablespoon picante sauce on each tortilla.

2. Sprinkle cheese, turkey ham and chilies equally over half of each tortilla; fold over uncovered half to make quesadilla; spray tops and bottoms with cooking spray.

3. Grill on uncovered grill over medium coals 1½ minutes per side or until cheese is melted and tortillas are golden brown, turning once. Quarter each quesadilla and serve with additional picante sauce and fat-free sour cream, if desired.   *Makes 2 servings*

Chicken and Vegetable Tortilla Roll-Ups

Chicken and Black Bean Soft Tacos

1 package (10) ORTEGA® Soft Taco
  Dinner Kit (flour tortillas, taco
  seasoning mix and taco sauce)
1 tablespoon vegetable oil
1 pound (3 to 4) boneless, skinless chicken
  breast halves, cut into 2-inch strips
1 cup (1 small) chopped onion
1¾ cups (15-ounce can) black beans, drained
¾ cup whole kernel corn
½ cup water
2 tablespoons lime juice

HEAT oil in large skillet over medium-high heat. Add chicken and onion; cook 4 to 5 minutes or until chicken is no longer pink. Stir in taco seasoning mix, beans, corn, water and lime juice. Bring to a boil. Reduce heat to low; cook, stirring occasionally, 5 to 6 minutes or until mixture is thickened.

REMOVE tortillas from outer plastic pouch. Microwave at HIGH (100%) 10 to 15 seconds or until warm. Or heat each tortilla, turning frequently, in small skillet over medium-high heat until warm.

FILL tortillas with ½ cup chicken mixture and taco sauce. *Makes 10 tacos*

Thai Turkey Roll-Up

½ pound Roasted Turkey Breast, cut into
  ¼-inch strips
2 tablespoons crunchy peanut butter
2 tablespoons minced green onion
2 tablespoons reduced-sodium soy sauce
  Juice of 1 lime
1 tablespoon brown sugar
1 tablespoon minced cilantro
1 teaspoon minced garlic
1 teaspoon minced fresh gingerroot
½ teaspoon grated lime peel
¼ teaspoon red pepper flakes
1 loaf soft lavosh

1. In medium bowl, combine turkey strips, peanut butter, green onion, soy sauce, lime juice, brown sugar, cilantro, garlic, gingerroot, lime peel and red pepper flakes. Cover and refrigerate for at least 1 hour.

2. Unfold lavosh; drain turkey mixture, if necessary, and spread evenly along lower quarter of bread.

3. Fold in bottom and top portions. Roll up from side to completely enclose filling. Cut into four equal portions. *Makes 4 servings*

Cooking Tip: Lavosh is a round, thin bread that comes in both soft and crisp versions; it is available in Middle Eastern markets and in most supermarkets.

Favorite recipe from **National Turkey Federation**

Chicken and Black Bean Soft Tacos

Turkey Burritos

1 tablespoon ground cumin
1 tablespoon chili powder
1½ teaspoons salt
1½ to 2 pounds turkey tenderloin, cut into
    ½-inch cubes
Avocado-Corn Salsa (recipe follows,
    optional)
Lime wedges
Flour tortillas
Sour cream (optional)
Tomato slices for garnish

Combine cumin, chili powder and salt in cup. Place turkey cubes in a shallow glass dish or large heavy plastic bag; pour dry rub over turkey and coat turkey thoroughly. Let turkey stand while preparing Avocado-Corn Salsa. Thread turkey onto metal or bamboo skewers. (Soak bamboo skewers in water at least 20 minutes before using to prevent them from burning.)

Oil hot grid to help prevent sticking. Grill turkey, on a covered grill, over medium KINGSFORD® Briquets, about 6 minutes or until turkey is no longer pink in center, turning once. Remove skewers from grill; squeeze lime wedges over skewers. Warm flour tortillas in microwave oven, or brush each tortilla very lightly with water and grill 10 to 15 seconds per side. Top with Avocado-Corn Salsa and sour cream, if desired. Garnish with tomato slices.

Makes 6 servings

Avocado-Corn Salsa

2 small to medium-size ripe avocados, finely
    chopped
1 cup cooked fresh corn or thawed frozen
    corn
2 medium tomatoes, seeded and finely
    chopped
2 to 3 tablespoons chopped fresh cilantro
2 to 3 tablespoons lime juice
½ to 1 teaspoon minced hot green chili
    pepper*
½ teaspoon salt

*Chile peppers can sting and irritate the skin; wear rubber gloves when handling and do not touch eyes. Wash hands after handling.

Gently stir together all ingredients in medium bowl; adjust flavors to taste. Cover and refrigerate until ready to serve.

Makes about 1½ cups

Tip: This recipe is great for casual get-togethers. Just prepare the fixings and let the guests make their own burritos.

Chicken, Spinach & Raisin Enchiladas

2 boneless skinless chicken breasts
  (5 ounces each)
1 package (10 ounces) frozen chopped
  spinach, thawed, well drained
1½ cups (6 ounces) shredded reduced-fat
  Monterey Jack cheese, divided
¾ cup part-skim ricotta cheese
½ cup raisins or currants
¼ teaspoon ground cloves
12 (6-inch) corn tortillas
  Roasted Tomato Enchilada Sauce (recipe
  follows)

1. Preheat oven to 350°F.

2. Bring 4 cups water to a boil over high heat in large saucepan. Add chicken. Cover; remove from heat. Let stand 15 minutes or until chicken is no longer pink in center. Drain; cool slightly and tear into small pieces. Place spinach in large bowl with chicken, 1 cup Monterey Jack cheese, ricotta cheese, raisins and cloves; stir to combine.

3. Heat large nonstick skillet over medium-high heat. Place 1 inch water in medium bowl. Dip 1 tortilla in water; shake off excess. Place in hot skillet. Cook 10 to 15 seconds on each side or until tortilla is hot and pliable. Repeat with remaining tortillas.

4. Spray 13×9-inch baking dish with nonstick cooking spray. Place 1 cup Roasted Tomato Enchilada Sauce in large bowl. Dip tortillas 1 at a time into sauce; shake off excess. Spread ⅓ cup chicken mixture in center of each tortilla; fold sides over to enclose and place seam side down in pan. Spread remaining Enchilada Sauce over enchiladas. Cover pan tightly with foil.

5. Bake 30 to 40 minutes or until heated through. Sprinkle with remaining ½ cup Monterey Jack cheese. Bake 3 minutes or until cheese melts.   *Makes 6 servings*

Roasted Tomato Enchilada Sauce

2 pounds small tomatoes
1 red bell pepper
4 cloves garlic, unpeeled
2 teaspoons olive oil
1 small onion, chopped
1 tablespoon chili powder
½ teaspoon ground cinnamon
¼ teaspoon ground cloves

1. Place tomatoes, bell pepper and garlic on broiler pan. Broil 2 inches from heat 8 minutes or until vegetables are browned in spots. Turn vegetables; repeat 2 more times until vegetables are browned on all sides.

2. Place tomatoes in food processor. Peel skin from pepper; remove stem and seeds. Add pepper to tomatoes. Slice open garlic cloves and press into tomato mixture; process until smooth.

3. Heat oil over medium-high heat in large saucepan. Add onion; cook and stir 4 minutes or until tender. Add seasonings. Cook 1 minute more. Reduce heat to medium-low. Pour tomato mixture into pan; simmer, uncovered, 10 minutes or until hot.   *Makes 6 servings*

Chicken, Spinach & Raisin
Enchiladas

Chicken Enchiladas with Chile-Cilantro Sauce

CHILE-CILANTRO SAUCE
2 cups Green Chile-Cilantro Pesto (recipe follows)
1 cup chicken broth
1 cup heavy whipping cream

CHICKEN ENCHILADAS
1 tablespoon vegetable oil
1 small onion, quartered, sliced
3 cloves garlic, finely chopped
1 pound (3 to 4) boneless, skinless chicken breasts, cut into small pieces
1 cup (7-ounce can) ORTEGA® Diced Green Chiles
½ teaspoon each salt and ground cumin
¼ teaspoon ground black pepper
12 corn tortillas
2 cups (8 ounces) shredded Monterey Jack cheese

COMBINE Green Chile-Cilantro Pesto, broth and cream in medium bowl; mix well. Pour half of sauce onto bottom of 13×9-inch baking pan.

HEAT oil in large skillet over medium-high heat. Add onion and garlic; cook for 1 minute. Add chicken; cook, stirring frequently, for 4 to 5 minutes or until chicken is no longer pink. Stir in chiles, salt, cumin and pepper.

HEAT tortillas in small skillet over high heat for 30 to 40 seconds on each side. Top each with ¼ cup chicken mixture and 1 tablespoon cheese; roll up. Place in baking pan. Top with remaining sauce and remaining cheese. Bake, covered, in preheated 350°F. oven for 15 to 20 minutes or until heated through. *Makes 6 servings*

GREEN CHILE-CILANTRO PESTO:
COMBINE 2 cups fresh cilantro sprigs, 1 cup (7-ounce can) ORTEGA® Diced Green Chiles, 1 cup (4 ounces) grated Parmesan cheese, ¾ cup toasted pine nuts, 4 large cloves garlic and 1 tablespoon lime juice in food processor or blender container; cover. Process until well chopped. Process, while slowly adding ½ cup corn oil, for additional 20 to 30 seconds or until almost smooth.

Oven-Roasted Turkey Breast Fajitas

2 teaspoons vegetable oil
1 medium onion, sliced
1 cup green or red bell pepper strips (or combination)
4 kosher flour tortillas (6 or 7 inches), warmed
12 ounces HEBREW NATIONAL® Sliced Oven Roasted Turkey Breast
8 thin slices ripe avocado
¾ cup prepared salsa

Heat oil in small nonstick skillet over medium heat. Add onion and pepper strips; cook until tender. Fill each tortilla with 3 ounces turkey breast, ½ cup onion mixture, 2 slices avocado and 3 tablespoons salsa. Roll up tortilla; serve immediately. *Makes 4 servings*

Chicken Enchiladas with Chile-Cilantro Sauce

Blackened Chicken Salad in Pitas

1 tablespoon paprika
1 teaspoon onion powder
½ teaspoon garlic powder
½ teaspoon dried oregano leaves
½ teaspoon dried thyme leaves
¼ teaspoon salt
¼ teaspoon white pepper
¼ teaspoon ground red pepper
¼ teaspoon black pepper
2 boneless skinless chicken breast halves
     (about ¾ pound)
4 pita breads
1 cup bite-size pieces spinach leaves
2 small tomatoes, cut into 8 slices
8 thin slices cucumber
½ cup reduced-fat ranch dressing

1. Combine paprika, onion powder, garlic powder, oregano, thyme, salt and peppers in small bowl; rub on all surfaces of chicken. Grill chicken on covered grill over medium-hot coals, 10 minutes per side or until chicken is no longer pink in center. Cool slightly. Cut into thin strips.

2. Wrap 2 pita breads in paper towels. Microwave at High 20 to 30 seconds or just until warm. Repeat with remaining pita breads.

3. Divide spinach, chicken strips, tomato slices, cucumber slices and ranch dressing among pita breads. Fold edges over and secure with wooden picks. Serve warm.   *Makes 4 servings*

Garlicky Chicken Packets

1 cup julienned carrots
½ cup sliced onion
¼ cup chopped fresh basil *or* 1 tablespoon
     dried basil leaves
2 tablespoons mayonnaise
6 cloves garlic, minced
⅛ teaspoon black pepper
4 boneless skinless chicken breast halves

Cut parchment paper or foil into 4 (12-inch) squares. Fold squares in half, then cut into shape of half hearts. Open parchment to form hearts.

Preheat oven to 400°F. Place carrots and onion on 1 side of each heart near fold. Combine basil, mayonnaise, garlic and pepper in small bowl; spread mixture on chicken. Place chicken, mayonnaise side up, on top of vegetables. Fold parchment over chicken; seal by creasing and folding edges of parchment in small overlapping sections from top of heart until completed at point. Finish by twisting point and tucking under.

Place parchment packages on ungreased baking sheet. Bake 20 to 25 minutes or until juices run clear and chicken is no longer pink in center.
          Makes 4 servings

Blackened Chicken Salad in Pita

Chicken Phyllo Wraps

Vegetable cooking spray
1 pound ground chicken
1 cup chopped fresh mushrooms
1 medium onion, chopped
3 cups cooked rice (cooked without salt and fat)
1 cup nonfat low-salt ricotta cheese
1 package (10 ounces) chopped spinach, thawed and well drained
1 can (2¼ ounces) sliced black olives, drained
¼ cup pine nuts, toasted*
2 cloves garlic, minced
1 teaspoon ground oregano
1 teaspoon lemon pepper
12 phyllo dough sheets

*To toast nuts, place on baking sheet. Bake at 350°F 5 to 7 minutes or until lightly browned.

Coat large skillet with cooking spray; heat over medium-high heat until hot. Add chicken, mushrooms and onion; cook and stir 2 to 4 minutes or until chicken is no longer pink and vegetables are tender. Reduce heat to medium. Add remaining ingredients except phyllo; cook and stir 3 to 4 minutes until hot. Working with 1 phyllo sheet at a time, spray 1 sheet with cooking spray; fold sheet in half lengthwise. Place ¾ to 1 cup rice mixture on one end of phyllo strip. Fold left bottom corner over mixture, forming a triangle. Continue folding back and forth into triangle at end of strip. Repeat with remaining phyllo sheets and rice mixture. Place triangles, seam sides down, on baking sheets coated with cooking spray. Coat top of each triangle with cooking spray. Bake at 400°F 15 to 20 minutes or until golden brown. Serve immediately.   *Makes 12 servings*

Favorite recipe from **USA Rice Federation**

Mesquite Grilled Chicken en Croûte

¾ cup LAWRY'S® Mesquite Marinade with Lime Juice
4 boneless, skinless chicken breast halves
½ cup chopped red bell pepper
½ cup toasted pine nuts, finely chopped
¼ cup toasted walnuts, finely chopped (optional)
1 can (7 ounces) diced green chiles
1 tablespoon lime juice
½ teaspoon LAWRY'S® Seasoned Salt
½ teaspoon LAWRY'S® Garlic Powder with Parsley
1 package (11 ounces) refrigerated cornstick dough or refrigerated breadstick dough
1 egg white, beaten

In resealable plastic bag, combine Mesquite Marinade and chicken. Marinate in refrigerator 30 minutes. Grill over hot coals 5 minutes, just until no longer pink. In small bowl, combine red bell pepper, nuts, chiles, lime juice, Seasoned Salt and Garlic Powder with Parsley. Roll dough out into four equal squares. On each square place a chicken breast and equal portions of vegetable mixture. Fold dough over chicken and filling. Seal edges to enclose. Brush tops with egg white. Bake in 350°F oven 3 to 5 minutes until golden and puffy.   *Makes 4 servings*

Chicken Phyllo Wrap

Ya Gotta Empanada

1 package (4.4 to 6.8 ounces) Spanish rice
    mix, prepared according to directions
1 cup shredded cooked chicken
1 cup (4 ounces) shredded Cheddar cheese
½ cup sliced green onions
¼ cup chopped black olives
1 package (15 ounces) refrigerated pie crust

Combine rice, chicken, cheese, onions and olives in large bowl. Spoon half of rice mixture onto half of each pie crust. Fold crust over filling. Seal and crimp edges. Place on baking sheet. Bake at 400°F 20 to 22 minutes or until golden brown. Cut in half. *Makes 4 servings*

Favorite recipe from **USA Rice Federation**

Chicken Baked in Parchment

4 boneless skinless chicken breast halves
1 cup matchstick-size carrot strips
1 cup matchstick-size zucchini strips
½ cup snow peas
½ cup thinly sliced red bell pepper
2¼ cups chicken broth, divided
2 tablespoons all-purpose flour
2 cloves garlic, minced
½ teaspoon dried thyme leaves
¼ teaspoon salt
¼ teaspoon ground nutmeg
¼ teaspoon black pepper
1 package (6 ounces) wheat pilaf mix

1. Preheat oven to 375°F. Cut parchment paper into 4 (10-inch) squares. Place 1 chicken breast in center of each piece of parchment; arrange carrots, zucchini, peas and bell pepper around chicken.

2. Combine ½ cup chicken broth and flour in small saucepan; stir in garlic, thyme, salt, nutmeg and black pepper. Heat to a boil, stirring constantly, until thickened. Reduce heat to low; simmer 1 minute. Spoon broth mixture evenly over chicken and vegetables.

3. Fold each parchment square in half diagonally, enclosing chicken and vegetables to form a triangle. Fold edges over twice to seal. Place parchment packets on 15×10-inch jelly-roll pan. Bake 25 to 30 minutes or until parchment is browned and puffed.

4. Place remaining 1¾ cups chicken broth in medium saucepan. Heat to a boil over medium-high heat. Stir in pilaf mix (discard spice packet). Reduce heat to low and simmer, covered, 15 minutes or until broth is absorbed.

5. Arrange parchment packets on serving plates; open carefully. Serve with pilaf.
Makes 4 servings

Tempting
MEAT WRAPS

Chili-Garlic Steak Fajitas

1 sirloin steak (about 1 pound), cut into ¼-inch-thick strips
1 small onion, cut into thin wedges
1 small green bell pepper, cut into thin strips
2 tablespoons olive oil
1½ teaspoons bottled minced garlic
1½ teaspoons chili powder
1 can (10 ounces) diced tomatoes with chilies, drained
8 (6- or 7-inch) flour tortillas
1 cup (4 ounces) shredded Cheddar or Monterey Jack cheese

1. Combine steak, onion, bell pepper, oil, garlic and chili powder in large resealable plastic food storage bag. Seal bag and shake to evenly distribute marinade; refrigerate up to 1 day before cooking.

2. To complete recipe, heat large nonstick skillet over high heat until hot. Add steak and vegetable mixture with marinade; cook 3 minutes. Add tomatoes; cook 2 minutes for medium-rare steak or to desired doneness. Serve with tortillas and cheese.   *Makes 4 servings*

Make-ahead time: up to 1 day before cooking

Final prep and cook time: 8 minutes

Chili-Garlic Steak Fajitas

Cheese-Stuffed Beef Rolls

1 jar (15½ ounces) spaghetti sauce
1 egg, slightly beaten
¼ teaspoon dried oregano, crumbled
¼ teaspoon garlic powder
1 container (15 ounces) ricotta cheese
¼ cup (1 ounce) grated Parmesan cheese
1 cup (4 ounces) shredded mozzarella
    cheese, divided
1⅓ cups (2.8-ounce can) FRENCH'S®
    French Fried Onions, divided
6 thin slices deli roast beef (about ½ pound)
2 medium zucchini, sliced (about 3 cups)

Preheat oven to 375°F. Spread ½ cup spaghetti sauce in bottom of 12×8-inch baking dish. In large bowl, thoroughly combine egg, seasonings, ricotta cheese, Parmesan cheese, ½ cup mozzarella cheese and ⅔ cup French Fried Onions. Spoon equal amounts of cheese mixture on 1 end of each beef slice. Roll up beef slices jelly-roll style and arrange, seam-side down, in baking dish. Place zucchini along both sides of dish. Pour remaining spaghetti sauce over beef rolls and zucchini. Bake, covered, at 375°F for 40 minutes or until heated through. Top beef rolls with remaining ½ cup mozzarella cheese and remaining ⅔ cup onions. Bake, uncovered, 3 minutes or until onions are golden brown.

Makes 6 servings

Microwave Directions: In large microwave-safe bowl, prepare cheese mixture as above. Cook, covered, on HIGH 2 to 4 minutes or until warmed through. Stir cheese mixture halfway through cooking time. Spread ½ cup spaghetti sauce in bottom of 12×8-inch microwave-safe dish. Prepare beef rolls and place in dish as above. Arrange zucchini along both sides of dish. Pour remaining spaghetti sauce over beef rolls and zucchini. Cook, loosely covered, 14 to 16 minutes or until heated through. Rotate dish halfway through cooking time. Top beef rolls with remaining ½ cup mozzarella cheese and ⅔ cup onions; cook, uncovered, 1 minute or until cheese melts. Let stand 5 minutes.

Ranch-Style Fajitas

2 pounds flank or skirt steak
½ cup vegetable oil
⅓ cup lime juice
2 packages (1 ounce each) HIDDEN
    VALLEY® Milk Recipe Original
    Ranch® Salad Dressing Mix
1 teaspoon ground cumin
½ teaspoon black pepper
6 flour tortillas
    Lettuce
    Guacamole, prepared HIDDEN VALLEY®
    Salad Dressing and picante sauce for
    toppings

Place steak in large baking dish. In small bowl, whisk together oil, lime juice, salad dressing mix, cumin and pepper. Pour mixture over steak. Cover and refrigerate several hours or overnight.

Remove steak; place marinade in small saucepan. Bring to a boil. Grill steak over medium-hot coals 8 to 10 minutes or to desired doneness, turning once and basting with heated marinade during last 5 minutes of grilling. Remove steak and slice diagonally across grain into thin slices.

Heat tortillas following package directions. Divide steak strips among tortillas; roll up to enclose. Serve with lettuce and desired toppings.

Makes 6 servings

Original Ortega® Taco Recipe

1 pound ground beef
1 package (1.0 ounce) ORTEGA® Taco Seasoning Mix
¾ cup water
1 package (12) ORTEGA® Taco Shells or (12) ORTEGA® White Corn Taco Shells
1½ cups (6 ounces) shredded Cheddar cheese
2½ cups shredded lettuce
2 cups (2 medium) chopped tomatoes
ORTEGA® Thick & Smooth Taco Sauce

COOK beef in medium skillet over medium-high heat for 4 to 5 minutes or until no longer pink; drain. Stir in taco seasoning mix and water. Bring to a boil. Reduce heat to low; cook, stirring occasionally, for 5 to 6 minutes or until mixture is thickened. Remove taco shells from freshness pack. Heat shells in microwave oven on HIGH (100%) power for 40 to 60 seconds or place on baking sheet in preheated 350°F. oven for 5 to 6 minutes. Fill taco shells with 2 to 3 tablespoons beef mixture. Top with cheese, lettuce, tomatoes and taco sauce.

Makes 6 servings

Special Beef and Spinach Burritos

1 pound lean ground beef
1 small onion, chopped
1 clove garlic, crushed
½ teaspoon salt
½ teaspoon chili powder
¼ teaspoon ground cumin
¼ teaspoon black pepper
1 package (10 ounces) frozen chopped spinach, thawed, well drained
2 jalapeño peppers, seeded, finely chopped
1½ cups (6 ounces) shredded Monterey Jack cheese
4 large (10-inch) *or* 8 medium (8-inch) flour tortillas, warmed
Lime slices (optional)
Jalapeño pepper slices (optional)
1 cup prepared chunky salsa

In large nonstick skillet, brown beef, onion and garlic over medium heat 8 to 10 minutes or until beef is no longer pink, stirring occasionally. Pour off drippings. Season with salt, chili powder, cumin and black pepper. Stir in spinach and jalapeño peppers; heat through. Remove from heat; stir in cheese.

To serve, spoon equal amounts of beef mixture into center of each tortilla. Fold bottom edge up over filling. Fold right and left sides to center, overlapping edges. Garnish with lime and jalapeño slices, if desired. Serve with salsa.

Makes 4 servings

Favorite recipe from **North Dakota Beef Commission**

Moo Shu Beef

½ **pound deli roast beef, cut ⅛ inch thick**
1 **tablespoon dry sherry**
3 **teaspoons reduced-sodium soy sauce,**
    divided
2 **teaspoons cornstarch, divided**
1 **teaspoon minced fresh ginger**
1 **clove garlic, minced**
½ **teaspoon sugar**
¼ **cup cold water**
¼ **cup beef broth**
3 **tablespoons peanut or vegetable oil,**
    divided
1 **egg, lightly beaten**
1 **cup shredded carrots**
1 **can (8 ounces) sliced bamboo shoots,**
    drained and cut into thin strips
3 **green onions with tops, cut into ½-inch**
    pieces
  Hoisin or plum sauce
8 **(7-to 8-inches) flour tortillas, warmed**

1. Cut beef into thin strips. Combine sherry, 1 teaspoon soy sauce, 1 teaspoon cornstarch, ginger, garlic and sugar in large bowl; stir well. Add beef; toss to coat. Marinate 10 minutes.

2. Stir water, broth and remaining 2 teaspoons soy sauce into 1 teaspoon cornstarch in cup until smooth; set aside.

3. Heat wok over high heat until hot. Drizzle 1 tablespoon oil into wok; heat 30 seconds. Pour egg into wok; tilt to coat bottom. Stir egg, breaking into small pieces. Remove from wok.

4. Add remaining 2 tablespoons oil to wok and heat 30 seconds. Add carrots; stir-fry 1 minute.

Add beef mixture, bamboo shoots and green onions; stir-fry 1 minute. Stir broth mixture until smooth; add to wok. Cook and stir 1 minute or until sauce boils and thickens. Cook 1 minute more. Stir in egg.

5. Spread equal amount of hoisin sauce on each tortilla. Spoon beef mixture over sauce. Fold bottom of tortilla up over filling, then fold sides over filling. Transfer to serving plate.

Makes 4 servings

Reuben Roll-Ups

8 **(7-inch) flour tortillas**
¾ **cup FRENCH'S® Deli Brown® Mustard**
1 **pound sliced corned beef**
2 **cups (8 ounces) shredded Swiss cheese**
½ **cup sauerkraut**

Spread each tortilla with about 1½ tablespoons mustard. Layer corned beef, cheese and sauerkraut on tortillas, dividing evenly. Roll up tortillas jelly-roll style. Secure with toothpicks.*

Place tortillas on oiled barbecue grill grid. Grill over medium-low coals about 10 minutes or until tortillas are toasted and cheese begins to melt, turning often. Remove toothpicks before serving.

Makes 4 servings

*Soak toothpicks in water 20 minutes to prevent burning.

Prep Time: 20 minutes
Cook Time: 10 minutes

Moo Shu Beef

Steak & Pepper Fajitas

1 packet (1.12 ounces) fajita marinade
1 pound boneless steak,* cut into thin strips
1 bag (16 ounces) BIRDS EYE® frozen
   Farm Fresh Mixtures Pepper Stir Fry
   vegetables
8 (6- to 7-inch) flour tortillas, warmed
½ cup salsa

*Or, substitute 1 pound boneless, skinless chicken, cut into strips.

• Prepare fajita marinade according to package directions.

• Add steak and vegetables. Let stand 10 minutes.

• Heat large skillet over medium-high heat. Remove steak and vegetables from marinade with slotted spoon and place in skillet.

• Add marinade, if desired. Cook 5 minutes or until steak is desired doneness and mixture is heated through, stirring occasionally.

• Wrap mixture in tortillas. Top with salsa.
Makes 4 servings

Serving Suggestions: Serve with guacamole and sour cream, or serve mixture over rice instead of in flour tortillas.

Prep Time: 10 minutes
Cook Time: 5 to 7 minutes

Beef Chimichangas

1 package (8) ORTEGA® Burrito Dinner
   Kit (flour tortillas and burrito seasoning
   mix)
1 pound ground beef
1¾ cups water
1 cup (4 ounces) shredded Cheddar cheese
   Vegetable oil
   ORTEGA® Thick & Chunky Salsa, hot,
   medium or mild
   Sour cream (optional)
   Guacamole (optional)

COOK beef in medium skillet over medium-high heat for 4 to 5 minutes or until no longer pink; drain. Stir in burrito seasoning mix and water. Bring to a boil. Reduce heat to low; cook, stirring constantly, for 5 to 6 minutes or until mixture is thickened.

REMOVE tortillas from outer plastic pouch. Microwave on HIGH (100%) power for 10 to 15 seconds or until warm. Or heat each tortilla, turning frequently, in small skillet over medium-high heat until warm.

SPREAD beef mixture over tortillas; top with cheese. Fold into burritos, closing both ends; secure with toothpicks.

ADD oil to 1-inch depth in medium skillet; heat over high heat for 1 minute. Place burritos in oil; fry, turning frequently with tongs, until golden brown. Remove from skillet; place on paper towels. Remove toothpicks. Serve with salsa, sour cream and guacamole. *Makes 8 servings*

Vietnamese Grilled Steak Wraps

1 beef flank steak (about 1½ pounds)
Grated peel and juice of 2 lemons
6 tablespoons sugar, divided
2 tablespoons dark sesame oil
1¼ teaspoons salt, divided
½ teaspoon black pepper
¼ cup water
¼ cup rice vinegar
½ teaspoon crushed red pepper
6 (8-inch) flour tortillas
6 red leaf lettuce leaves
⅓ cup lightly packed fresh mint leaves
⅓ cup lightly packed fresh cilantro leaves
Star fruit slices
Red bell pepper strips
Orange peel strips

Cut beef across the grain into thin slices. Combine lemon peel, juice, 2 tablespoons sugar, sesame oil, 1 teaspoon salt and black pepper in medium bowl. Add beef; toss to coat. Cover and refrigerate at least 30 minutes. Combine water, vinegar, remaining 4 tablespoons sugar and ¼ teaspoon salt in small saucepan; bring to a boil. Boil 5 minutes without stirring until syrupy. Stir in crushed red pepper; set aside.

Remove beef from marinade; discard marinade. Thread beef onto metal or wooden skewers. (Soak wooden skewers in hot water 30 minutes to prevent burning.) Grill beef over medium-hot KINGSFORD® briquets about 3 minutes per side until cooked through. Grill tortillas until hot. Place lettuce, beef, mint and cilantro on tortillas;

drizzle with vinegar mixture. Roll tortillas to enclose filling. Garnish with star fruit, bell pepper and orange peel strips. *Makes 6 wraps*

Guadalajara Beef

1 bottle (12 ounces) dark beer
¼ cup low-sodium soy sauce
3 cloves garlic, minced
1 teaspoon ground cumin
1 teaspoon ground chili powder
½ teaspoon ground red pepper
1 pound beef flank steak
6 medium bell peppers, seeded and cut lengthwise into quarters
8 (6- to 8-inch) flour tortillas

1. Combine beer, soy sauce, garlic, cumin, chili powder and red pepper in resealable plastic food storage bag; add beef and seal. Refrigerate up to 1 day, turning occasionally.

2. To complete recipe, remove beef from marinade; discard remaining marinade. Grill beef over hot coals 7 minutes per side or until desired doneness. Grill bell peppers 7 to 10 minutes or until tender, turning once.

3. Slice beef and serve with bell peppers and tortillas. *Makes 4 servings*

Serving Suggestion: Serve beef with sour cream and salsa.

Make-ahead time: Up to 1 day before serving

Final prep time: 20 minutes

Vietnamese Grilled Steak Wrap

Double Duty Tacos

MEXICALI CHILI RUB

¼ cup chili powder
3 tablespoons garlic salt
2 tablespoons ground cumin
2 tablespoons dried oregano leaves
½ teaspoon ground red pepper

TACOS

2 pounds lean ground beef
1 large onion, chopped
3 tablespoons Mexicali Chili Rub
2 tablespoons tomato paste
16 packaged crispy taco shells
2 cups (8 ounces) shredded Monterey Jack cheese
2 cups shredded lettuce
1 cup chopped fresh tomatoes
1 cup diced ripe avocado
½ cup light or regular sour cream
Salsa

1. For rub, combine chili powder, garlic salt, cumin, oregano and ground red pepper in small bowl; mix well. Transfer to container with tight-fitting lid. Store in cool dry place up to 2 months.

2. Cook beef and onion in large deep skillet over medium-high heat until no longer pink; pour off drippings. Sprinkle chili rub over beef mixture; cook 1 minute. Reduce heat to medium.

3. Add ¾ cup water and tomato paste. Cover; simmer 5 minutes.

4. Spoon beef mixture into taco shells; top with cheese. Arrange lettuce, tomatoes, avocado, sour cream and salsa in bowls. Serve tacos with toppings as desired. *Makes 8 servings*

Serving Suggestion: Serve tacos with refried beans and Spanish rice.

Carne Asada

1½ to 1¾ pounds flank or boneless sirloin tip steak
½ cup lime juice
6 cloves garlic, chopped
1 teaspoon ground black pepper
Salt
1 large green bell pepper, cut lengthwise into 1-inch strips
8 corn tortillas, warmed
Salsa

1. Combine steak, lime juice, garlic and black pepper in large resealable plastic freezer bag; seal. Refrigerate overnight, turning at least once.

2. Preheat broiler. Remove steak from bag and place on broiler pan. Sprinkle with salt to taste. Add bell pepper to same bag; seal. Turn to coat with marinade; set aside. Broil steak 5 to 7 minutes per side or until well-browned, turning once. Add bell pepper to broiler pan; broil until softened.

3. Transfer steak to cutting board; slice across the grain into thin strips. Place steak on warm tortillas. Top with bell pepper and salsa. Serve immediately. *Makes 4 servings*

Double Duty Tacos

Speedy Beef & Bean Burritos

8 (7-inch) flour tortillas
1 pound ground beef
1 cup chopped onion (from the salad bar or frozen)
1 teaspoon bottled minced garlic
1 can (15 ounces) black beans, drained and rinsed
1 cup spicy thick-and-chunky salsa
2 teaspoons ground cumin
1 bunch cilantro
2 cups (8 ounces) shredded cojack or Monterey Jack cheese

1. Wrap tortillas in foil; place on center rack in oven. Turn temperature to 350°F; heat tortillas 15 minutes.

2. While tortillas are warming, prepare burrito filling. Combine meat, onion and garlic in large skillet; cook over medium-high heat until meat is no longer pink, breaking meat apart with wooden spoon. Pour off drippings.

3. Stir beans, salsa and cumin into meat mixture; reduce heat to medium. Cover and simmer 10 minutes, stirring once.

4. While filling is simmering, chop enough cilantro to measure ¼ cup. Stir into filling. Spoon filling down centers of warm tortillas; top with cheese. Roll up and serve immediately.
Makes 4 servings

Prep and Cook Time: 20 minutes

Calzone Mexicana

1 package (1.0 ounce) LAWRY'S® Taco Spices & Seasonings
1 pound ground beef
¾ cup water
All-purpose flour
1 pound frozen bread dough, thawed, *or* 2 cans (9 ounces each) refrigerated pizza dough
2 cups (8 ounces) shredded Monterey Jack cheese
1 can (4 ounces) diced green chilies, drained
Dairy sour cream for garnish
Salsa (garnish)

Heat oven to 350°F. Prepare Taco Spices & Seasonings with ground beef and water according to package directions; set aside. On floured board, roll out dough to 14×8-inch rectangle. Spread taco meat mixture onto center of dough, leaving 2-inch border. Layer cheese and chilies on top. Fold dough lengthwise in half; pinch edges together to seal. Place on lightly greased baking sheet. Bake, uncovered, 30 minutes or until golden brown. *Makes 4 to 6 servings*

Presentation: Cut into slices and top with sour cream and salsa, if desired.

Tip: For extra flavor, brush top of calzone with beaten egg and lightly sprinkle with cornmeal before baking.

Variation: For four individual calzones, cut rolled dough into four equal rectangles. Fill and fold as directed above. Place on lightly greased baking sheet. Bake at 350°F 20 minutes or until golden brown.

Speedy Beef & Bean Burritos

Italian Sausage & Pepper Pita Wraps

4 (6-inch) hot or mild Italian sausages (about 1¼ pounds)
1 green bell pepper, cut lengthwise into quarters, stems and seeds discarded
1 small onion, sliced
1 cup prepared marinara sauce
½ teaspoon dried basil leaves
¼ teaspoon dried oregano leaves
4 pita breads
1 tablespoon olive oil
1 cup (4 ounces) shredded Italian blend cheese or mozzarella cheese

1. Prepare grill for direct cooking.

2. Place sausage links on center of grid over medium coals; arrange bell pepper and onion around sausages. Grill on covered grill 7 minutes. Turn sausages and vegetables; grill 8 to 9 minutes or until sausages are cooked through and vegetables are crisp-tender.

3. Brush pita breads on one side with oil. Place on grid at edge of coals; grill until soft.

4. Meanwhile, combine marinara sauce, basil and oregano in small saucepan. Simmer over medium-low heat until hot, about 5 minutes.

5. Cut sausages in half lengthwise. Cut bell pepper into strips and separate onion slices into rings.

6. Divide sausages, bell pepper and onion among pita breads. Top with sauce and cheese. Fold pita breads in half. *Makes 4 servings*

Oriental-Style Ground Pork

1 package (8 ounces) shredded carrots
1 tablespoon sugar
1 teaspoon distilled white vinegar or rice vinegar
2 green onions with tops
1 teaspoon cornstarch
½ teaspoon chili powder
¼ cup chicken broth
1 tablespoon reduced-sodium soy sauce
1 tablespoon vegetable oil
1 pound ground pork
8 large mushrooms
Boston lettuce leaves

1. Combine carrots, sugar and vinegar in medium bowl; set aside.

2. Slice green onions diagonally into 1-inch pieces.

3. Combine cornstarch and chili powder in small bowl. Stir broth and soy sauce into cornstarch mixture until smooth. Set aside.

4. Heat wok over medium-high heat 1 minute or until hot. Drizzle oil into wok and heat 30 seconds. Add pork; stir-fry until well browned. Add mushrooms; stir-fry until tender.

5. Stir broth mixture until smooth and add to wok. Cook until sauce boils and thickens. Add green onions; cook 1 minute.

6. Line serving plate with lettuce leaves. Arrange carrot mixture in layer over leaves. Top with pork mixture. (Traditionally, the lettuce leaves are eaten as a wrapper to hold the ground meat mixture.) *Makes 4 servings*

Italian Sausage & Pepper Pita Wrap

Tacos

1 pound BOB EVANS® Original Recipe or
  Zesty Hot Roll Sausage
1 (8-ounce) jar taco sauce
1 package taco shells (10 to 12 count)
2 cups (8 ounces) shredded Cheddar cheese
1 large onion, chopped
2 tomatoes, chopped
¼ head iceberg lettuce, shredded
  Fresh cilantro sprigs and bell pepper
    triangles (optional)

Preheat oven to 350°F. Crumble sausage into
medium skillet; cook over medium-high heat
until browned, stirring occasionally. Drain off
any drippings. Stir in taco sauce. Bring to a boil.
Reduce heat to low; simmer 5 minutes.
Meanwhile, bake taco shells until warm and
crisp. To assemble tacos, place 2 tablespoons
sausage mixture in each taco shell and top evenly
with cheese, onion, tomatoes and lettuce.
Garnish with cilantro and pepper triangles, if
desired. Serve hot. Refrigerate any leftover
filling.   *Makes 10 to 12 servings*

Thai Pork Burritos

1 pound lean ground pork
2 tablespoons grated fresh ginger root
1 clove garlic, peeled and crushed
2 cups coleslaw mix with carrots
1 small onion, thinly sliced
3 tablespoons soy sauce
2 tablespoons lime juice
1 tablespoon honey
2 teaspoons ground coriander
1 teaspoon sesame oil
½ teaspoon crushed red pepper
4 large (10-inch) flour tortillas, warmed
  Fresh cilantro, chopped (optional)

Heat large nonstick skillet over high heat. Add
pork; cook and stir until pork is no longer pink, 3
to 4 minutes. Stir in ginger and garlic. Add
coleslaw mix and onion and stir-fry with pork for
2 minutes, until vegetables are wilted. Combine
all remaining ingredients except tortillas and
cilantro in small bowl and add to skillet. Stir
constantly to blend all ingredients well, about 1
minute. Spoon equal portions of mixture onto
warm flour tortillas and garnish with cilantro, if
desired. Roll up to encase filling and serve.
                            Makes 4 servings

Preparation Time: 15 minutes

Favorite recipe from **National Pork Producers Council**

Grilled Pork Soft Tacos

4 dried mild red ancho or California chiles,
  seeds and stems removed
¼ cup lime juice
3 tablespoons cold water
2 tablespoons olive oil, divided
2 cloves garlic, minced and divided
½ teaspoon salt, divided
½ teaspoon ground cumin
¼ cup reduced-fat sour cream
1½ pounds boneless pork loin chops, about
  ¾-inch thick
1 large red onion, cut into ¾-inch-thick
  slices
2 poblano or green bell peppers, cut in half,
  stemmed and seeded
1 large red bell pepper, cut in half, stemmed
  and seeded
6 corn tortillas
  Guacamole (optional)

Cover chiles with boiling water in small bowl.
Let stand 10 minutes; drain. Place chiles, lime
juice, water, 1 tablespoon oil, 1 clove garlic, ¼
teaspoon salt and cumin in blender; process until
smooth. Spoon half of chile mixture into small
bowl; stir in sour cream. Cover and refrigerate.
Spoon remaining chile mixture into 2-quart glass
dish; add remaining clove garlic and ¼ teaspoon
salt. Add pork, turning to coat. Cover and
refrigerate overnight. Brush onion slices with
remaining 1 tablespoon oil. Remove pork from
marinade; discard marinade. Grill pork and onion
over medium-hot KINGSFORD® briquets about
4 minutes per side until pork is barely pink. Grill
bell peppers, skin side down, 8 minutes until
skins are charred. Place peppers in large
resealable plastic food storage bag; seal. Let stand
5 minutes; remove skins. Grill tortillas until hot.
Slice pork, onion and peppers. Spoon sour cream
mixture down center of each tortilla; top with
pork, vegetables and guacamole, if desired. Fold
tortillas around filling. *Makes 6 tacos*

Border Scramble

1 pound BOB EVANS® Original Recipe
  Roll Sausage
1½ cups chopped cooked potatoes
1½ cups chopped onions
1½ cups chopped tomatoes
¾ cup chopped green bell pepper
¼ to ½ cup picante sauce
½ to 1 tablespoon hot pepper sauce
½ teaspoon garlic powder
½ teaspoon salt
4 (9-inch) flour tortillas
2 cups prepared meatless chili
½ cup (2 ounces) shredded Cheddar cheese

Crumble sausage into large skillet. Cook over
medium heat until browned, stirring occasionally.
Drain off any drippings. Add all remaining
ingredients except tortillas, chili and cheese;
simmer 20 minutes or until vegetables are crisp-
tender. To warm tortillas, microwave 1 minute at
HIGH between paper towels. Place 1 cup sausage
mixture in center of each tortilla; fold tortilla
over filling to close. Heat chili in small saucepan
until hot, stirring occasionally. Top each folded
tortilla with ½ cup chili and 2 tablespoons
cheese. Serve hot. Refrigerate leftovers.

Makes 4 servings

Pork Burritos

  1 boneless fresh pork butt roast
      (about 2½ pounds)
  1 cup chopped white onion
  1 carrot, sliced
  1 clove garlic, minced
  ½ teaspoon salt
  ½ teaspoon ground cumin
  ½ teaspoon coriander seeds, lightly crushed
 12 (8-inch) flour tortillas
  2 cups refried beans, heated
     Salsa
  2 medium firm, ripe avocados, diced
  1 cup (4 ounces) shredded Monterey Jack
      cheese
     Carrot sticks, avocado slices and cilantro
       sprig for garnish

Place pork, onion, carrot, garlic, salt, cumin and coriander seeds in 5-quart Dutch oven. Add just enough water to cover pork. Bring to a boil over high heat. Reduce heat to low. Cover and simmer 2 to 2½ hours until pork is tender.

Preheat oven to 350°F. Remove pork from Dutch oven; set aside. Strain cooking liquid through cheesecloth-lined sieve; reserve ½ cup liquid. Place pork in roasting pan. Roast 40 to 45 minutes until well browned, turning once. Let stand until cool enough to handle. Trim and discard outer fat from pork. Using 2 forks, pull pork into coarse shreds. Combine pork and reserved cooking liquid in medium skillet. Heat over medium heat 5 minutes or until meat is hot and coated with liquid; stirring often.

Stack tortillas and wrap in foil. Heat tortillas in 350°F oven 10 minutes or until warm. Spread about 2½ tablespoons beans onto each tortilla. Layer with pork, salsa, diced avocados and cheese. To form, fold right edge of tortilla up over filling; fold bottom edge over filling; then loosely roll up, leaving left end of burrito open. Garnish, if desired. *Makes 6 servings*

Fantastic Pork Fajitas

  1 pound pork strips
  2 teaspoons vegetable oil
  ½ medium onion, peeled and sliced
  1 green bell pepper, seeded and sliced
  4 flour tortillas, warmed
     Salsa (optional)

Heat large nonstick skillet over medium-high heat. Add oil; heat until hot. Add pork strips, onion and bell pepper slices to skillet and stir-fry quickly 4 to 5 minutes. Roll up portions of the meat mixture in flour tortillas and serve with purchased salsa, if desired. *Makes 4 servings*

Favorite recipe from **National Pork Producers Council**

Lasagne Roll-Ups

1 pound mild Italian sausage, casings
   removed
½ cup chopped onion
1 clove garlic, minced
1⅓ cups (12-ounce can) CONTADINA®
   Tomato Paste
1⅔ cups water
1 teaspoon dried oregano leaves, crushed
½ teaspoon dried basil leaves, crushed
1 egg
1 package (10 ounces) frozen chopped
   spinach, thawed, squeezed dry
2 cups (15-ounce container) ricotta cheese
1½ cups (6 ounces) shredded mozzarella
   cheese, divided
1 cup (4 ounces) grated Parmesan cheese
½ teaspoon salt
¼ teaspoon ground black pepper
8 dry lasagne noodles, cooked, drained, kept
   warm

In large skillet, crumble sausage. Add onion and garlic; cook until sausage is no longer pink. Drain. Stir in tomato paste, water, oregano and basil; cover. Bring to a boil. Reduce heat to low; simmer, uncovered, for 20 minutes. In medium bowl, beat egg lightly. Add spinach, ricotta cheese, 1 cup mozzarella cheese, Parmesan cheese, salt and pepper. Spread about ½ cup cheese mixture onto each noodle; roll up. Place, seam side down, in 12×7½-inch baking dish. Pour sauce over rolls; top with remaining mozzarella cheese. Bake in preheated 350°F oven for 30 to 40 minutes or until heated through.

Makes 8 servings

Shredded Pork Tacos

3 cups shredded or finely chopped cooked
   roast pork
1 cup chopped onion
1 clove garlic, minced
1 to 3 tablespoons diced jalapeño pepper
12 small flour tortillas, warmed
3 cups shredded lettuce
2 cups diced tomatoes
¾ cup (3 ounces) shredded Cheddar cheese
   Salsa (optional)

In medium nonstick skillet, cook and stir onion and garlic over medium heat 5 minutes until soft and translucent. Add cooked pork; toss lightly. Heat thoroughly; stir in jalapeño pepper. Onto each tortilla, spoon a scant ⅓ cup shredded pork mixture, a portion of lettuce, tomatoes and 1 tablespoon cheese; top with salsa, if desired.

Makes 6 servings

Preparation Time: 15 minutes

Favorite recipe from **National Pork Producers Council**

Lasagne Roll-Up

Calzone Italiano

Pizza dough for one 14-inch pizza
1¾ cups (15-ounce can) CONTADINA®
    Pizza Sauce, divided
3 ounces sliced pepperoni *or* ½ pound
    crumbled Italian sausage, cooked,
    drained
2 tablespoons chopped green bell pepper
1 cup (4 ounces) shredded mozzarella
    cheese
1 cup (8 ounces) ricotta cheese

Divide dough into 4 equal portions. Place on lightly floured, large, rimless cookie sheet. Press or roll out dough to 7-inch circles. Spread 2 tablespoons pizza sauce onto half of each circle to within ½ inch of edge; top with ¼ each pepperoni, bell pepper and mozzarella cheese. Spoon ¼ cup ricotta cheese onto remaining half of each circle; fold dough over. Press edges together tightly to seal. Cut slits in top of dough to allow steam to escape. Bake in preheated 350°F oven for 20 to 25 minutes or until crusts are golden brown. Meanwhile, heat remaining pizza sauce; serve over calzones.

Makes 4 servings

Note: If desired, 1 large calzone may be made instead of 4 individual calzones. To prepare, shape dough into 1 (13-inch) circle. Spread ½ cup pizza sauce onto half of dough; proceed as above. Bake for 25 minutes.

Welsh Pork Pasties

½ pound pork, cut into ½-inch cubes
½ cup onion, diced
¼ cup margarine
 1 teaspoon dried thyme
½ teaspoon salt
¼ teaspoon pepper
¼ cup all-purpose flour
 1 (12-ounce) can chicken broth
 1 (15-ounce) can VEG-ALL® Mixed
    Vegetables, drained
 2 (9-inch) refrigerated pie crusts
 1 egg beaten with 2 tablespoons milk

1. Cook and stir pork and onion in margarine for 15 minutes over medium high heat.

2. Add seasonings to meat mixture; sprinkle flour over meat mixture and cook until brown.

3. Add chicken broth. Blend until thickened and well combined.

4. Add Veg-All®. Mix well.

5. Remove from heat and chill until firm.

6. Lay out pie dough and cut 2 (9-inch) rounds in half.

7. Place ½ cup filling on each half circle. Fold in half and seal; crimp each pastie with decorative edge.

8. Brush with egg wash and milk mixture; pierce tops with fork and bake at 400°F until golden, about 20 minutes.

Makes 4 servings

Calzone Italiano

Mushroom Sausage Spinach Strudel

½ pound BOB EVANS® Original Recipe
    Roll Sausage
3 tablespoons olive oil
1 small onion, chopped
¼ pound fresh mushrooms, sliced
¼ cup chopped red bell pepper
1 clove garlic, minced
½ pound fresh spinach, washed, torn into
    small pieces and drained
¼ cup (1 ounce) shredded Swiss cheese
    Salt and black pepper to taste
4 sheets phyllo dough, thawed according to
    package directions
¼ cup butter or margarine, melted
3 tablespoons dry bread crumbs
    Fresh thyme sprig and red pepper strips
    (optional)

Crumble sausage into medium skillet. Cook over medium-high heat until browned, stirring occasionally. Drain off any drippings. Remove sausage to paper towels; set aside. Heat oil in same skillet. Add onion, mushrooms, chopped bell pepper and garlic; cook and stir until soft. Stir in sausage, spinach, cheese, salt and black pepper; cook until vegetables are tender. Set aside.

Preheat oven to 375°F. Place 1 phyllo sheet on work surface. Brush sheet with some melted butter; sprinkle with ¼ of bread crumbs. (Cover remaining sheets with damp kitchen towel.) Repeat layers three times. Spread sausage mixture over top; roll up, starting at one short side.

Place on ungreased baking sheet. Brush with remaining butter; bake 15 minutes or until golden. Let stand 5 minutes. Cut into slices. Garnish with thyme and pepper strips, if desired.
Makes 4 to 6 servings

Ham and Cheese Calzones

1 pound frozen bread dough, thawed
1 cup bottled marinara sauce
2 tablespoons low-sodium tomato paste
1 tablespoon slivered fresh basil leaves *or*
    1 teaspoon dried basil
1 cup (4 ounces) slivered ALPINE LACE®
    Boneless Cooked Ham
1½ cups (6 ounces) shredded ALPINE
    LACE® Fat Free Pasteurized Process
    Skim Milk Cheese Product—For
    Mozzarella Lovers
1 cup cooked small broccoli florets, drained
½ cup finely chopped red onion

1. Preheat the oven to 425°F. Spray 2 baking sheets with nonstick cooking spray. On a lightly floured surface, cut the dough into 6 equal pieces. Roll each piece into a 6-inch circle.

2. In a small bowl, blend the marinara sauce, the tomato paste and basil. Leaving a ½-inch border, spread the sauce over half of each dough circle. Sprinkle with the ham, cheese and vegetables.

3. Moisten the edges of the dough with a little water, fold the dough over filling and seal with a fork. Place on the baking sheets. Bake at 450°F for 10 minutes. Serve hot!   *Makes 6 calzones*

Mushroom Sausage Spinach Strudel

Middle Eastern Souvlaki

3 pounds lean boneless leg of lamb, cut into
   1-inch cubes
¾ cup prepared olive oil vinaigrette salad
   dressing
¼ cup FRANK'S® Original REDHOT®
   Cayenne Pepper Sauce
¼ cup FRENCH'S® Worcestershire Sauce
1 cup fresh mint leaves, coarsely chopped
1 tablespoon fennel or anise seeds, crushed
3 cloves garlic, minced
   Pita bread, cut in half crosswise
   Chopped tomatoes
   Sliced onions

YOGURT SAUCE
¾ cup plain nonfat yogurt
½ cup finely chopped cucumber
1 tablespoon FRANK'S® Original
   REDHOT® Cayenne Pepper Sauce
1 clove garlic, minced

Place lamb cubes in large resealable plastic food storage bag. Combine salad dressing, ¼ cup RedHot® sauce, Worcestershire, mint, fennel seeds and garlic in small bowl; mix well. Pour over lamb. Seal bag and marinate in refrigerator 1 hour.

To prepare Yogurt Sauce, combine yogurt, cucumber, 1 tablespoon RedHot® sauce and garlic in small bowl; set aside.

Thread lamb onto metal skewers, reserving marinade. Place skewers on grid. Grill over hot coals 10 to 15 minutes or to desired doneness, turning and basting often with marinade. (Do not baste during last 5 minutes of cooking.) To serve, remove lamb from skewers. Place lamb in pita bread halves. Top with tomatoes, onions and some of the Yogurt Sauce. Garnish as desired.

Makes 6 to 8 servings

Prep Time: 20 minutes
Marinate Time: 1 hour
Cook Time: 15 minutes

Middle Eastern Souvlaki

Superb
SEAFOOD WRAPS

Ensenada Fish Tacos

10 ounces halibut or orange roughy fillets,
    cut into 1-inch cubes
1 tablespoon vegetable oil
1 tablespoon lime juice
1 package (1.27 ounces) LAWRY'S® Spices
    & Seasonings for Fajitas
6 corn or flour tortillas (about 8 inches)
2½ cups shredded lettuce
½ cup diced tomatoes
¾ cup (3 ounces) shredded Monterey Jack
    or cheddar cheese
2 tablespoons thinly sliced green onion
    Dairy sour cream (optional)
    Guacamole (optional)
    Salsa (optional)
    Chopped fresh cilantro (optional)

In shallow glass baking dish, place fish. Pour oil and lime juice over fish. Sprinkle with Spices & Seasonings for Fajitas; toss lightly to coat. Cover. Refrigerate 2 hours to marinate, occasionally spooning marinade over fish. In same dish, bake fish in 450°F oven 10 minutes or until fish flakes easily with fork; drain. To serve, evenly divide fish; place in center of each tortilla. Top with lettuce, tomatoes, cheese and green onion.

Makes 6 servings

Serving Suggestion: Garnish with sour cream, guacamole, salsa and cilantro, to taste.

Ensenada Fish Tacos

Seafood Crêpes

Basic Crêpes (recipe follows)
3 tablespoons butter or margarine
⅓ cup finely chopped shallots or sweet onion
2 tablespoons dry vermouth
3 tablespoons all-purpose flour
1½ cups plus 2 tablespoons milk, divided
¼ to ½ teaspoon hot pepper sauce (optional)
8 ounces cooked peeled and deveined
    shrimp, coarsely chopped (1½ cups)
8 ounces lump crabmeat or imitation
    crabmeat, shredded (1½ cups)
2 tablespoons snipped fresh chives or green
    onion tops
3 tablespoons freshly grated Parmesan
    cheese
Fresh chives and red onion for garnish

1. Prepare Basic Crêpes. Preheat oven to 350°F.

2. Melt butter over medium heat in medium saucepan. Add shallots; cook and stir 5 minutes or until shallots are tender. Add vermouth; cook 1 minute.

3. Add flour; cook and stir 1 minute. Gradually stir in 1½ cups milk and hot pepper sauce, if desired. Bring to a boil, stirring frequently. Reduce heat to low; cook and stir 1 minute or until mixture thickens.

4. Remove from heat; stir in shrimp and crabmeat. Reserve ½ cup seafood mixture; set aside.

5. To assemble crêpes, spoon about ¼ cup seafood mixture down center of each crêpe. Roll up crêpes jelly-roll style. Place seam side down in well-greased 13×9-inch baking dish.

6. Stir chives and remaining 2 tablespoons milk into reserved seafood mixture. Spoon seafood mixture down center of crêpes; sprinkle cheese evenly over top.

7. Bake uncovered 15 to 20 minutes or until heated through. *Makes 6 servings*

Basic Crêpes

1½ cups milk
1 cup all-purpose flour
2 eggs
¼ cup butter or margarine, melted and
    cooled, divided
¼ teaspoon salt

1. Combine milk, flour, eggs, 2 tablespoons butter and salt in food processor; process using on/off pulsing action until smooth. Let stand at room temperature 30 minutes.

2. Heat ½ teaspoon butter in 7- or 8-inch crêpe pan or skillet over medium heat. Pour ¼ cup batter into pan. Immediately rotate pan to swirl batter over entire surface of pan.

3. Cook 1 to 2 minutes or until crêpe is brown around edges and top is dry. Carefully turn crêpe with spatula and cook 30 seconds more. Transfer crêpe to waxed paper to cool. Repeat with remaining batter, adding remaining butter only as needed to prevent sticking.

4. Separate each crêpe with sheet of waxed paper. Cover and refrigerate up to 1 day or freeze up to 1 month before serving.

Makes about 1 dozen crêpes

Tuna Fiesta Soft Tacos

⅓ cup mayonnaise
½ teaspoon garlic salt
½ teaspoon lemon pepper seasoning
1 can (6 ounces) STARKIST® Solid White or Chunk Light Tuna, drained and flaked
¼ cup chopped celery
1 hard-cooked egg, chopped
2 tablespoons finely chopped green onion
2 tablespoons finely chopped green bell pepper
1 tablespoon drained chopped pimiento
6 flour tortillas (6 inches each), warmed
1 cup shredded iceberg lettuce
½ cup shredded Colby or Monterey Jack cheese
   Salsa (optional)

In large bowl, combine mayonnaise, garlic salt, lemon pepper seasoning, tuna, celery, egg, onion, bell pepper and pimiento; mix thoroughly. Place generous ¼ cup filling on one side of each tortilla; top with lettuce and cheese. Fold tortilla over; serve with salsa, if desired.

Makes 6 servings

Tuna Tortilla Roll-Ups

1 can (10¾ ounces) condensed cream of celery soup
1 cup milk
1 can (9¼ ounces) tuna, drained and flaked
1 package (10 ounces) frozen broccoli spears, thawed, drained and cut into 1-inch pieces
1 cup (4 ounces) shredded Cheddar cheese
1⅓ cups (2.8-ounce can) FRENCH'S® French Fried Onions
6 (7-inch) flour or corn tortillas
1 medium tomato, chopped

Preheat oven to 350°F. In small bowl, combine soup and milk. In medium bowl, combine tuna, broccoli, ½ cup cheese and ⅔ *cup* French Fried Onions; stir in ¾ cup soup mixture. Divide tuna mixture among tortillas; roll up tortillas. Place, seam side down, in greased 13×9-inch baking dish. Stir tomato into remaining soup mixture; pour down center of roll-ups. Bake, covered, at 350°F for 35 minutes or until heated through. Top roll-ups with remaining cheese and ⅔ *cup* onions; bake, uncovered, 5 minutes or until onions are golden.

Makes 6 servings

Microwave Directions: Use corn tortillas only. Prepare soup mixture and roll-ups as above, placing roll-ups in 12×8-inch microwave-safe dish. Stir tomato into remaining soup mixture; pour down center of roll-ups. Cook, covered, on HIGH 15 to 18 minutes or until heated through. Rotate dish halfway through cooking time. Top roll-ups with remaining cheese and ⅔ *cup* onions; cook, uncovered, 1 minute or until cheese melts. Let stand 5 minutes.

Tuna Fiesta Soft Taco

Seafood Tacos with Fruit Salsa

2 tablespoons lemon juice
1 teaspoon chili powder
1 teaspoon ground allspice
1 teaspoon olive oil
1 teaspoon minced garlic
1 to 2 teaspoons grated lemon peel
½ teaspoon ground cloves
1 pound halibut or snapper fillets
12 (6-inch) corn tortillas or 6 (7- to 8-inch) flour tortillas
3 cups shredded romaine lettuce
1 small red onion, halved, thinly sliced
Fruit Salsa (recipe follows)

1. Combine lemon juice, chili powder, allspice, oil, garlic, lemon peel and cloves in small bowl. Rub fish with spice mixture; cover and refrigerate while grill heats, or refrigerate up to several hours. (Fish may be cut into smaller pieces for easier handling.)

2. Spray cold grid with nonstick cooking spray. Adjust grid 4 to 6 inches above heat. Preheat grill to medium-high heat. Grill fish, covered, 3 minutes or until fish is lightly seared on bottom. Carefully turn fish over; grill 2 minutes or until fish is opaque in center and flakes easily when tested with fork. Remove from heat and cut into 12 pieces, removing bones if necessary. Cover to keep warm.

3. Place tortillas on grill in single layer and cook 5 to 10 seconds; turn over and cook another 5 to 10 seconds or until hot and pliable. Stack; cover to keep warm.

4. Top each tortilla with ¼ cup lettuce and red onion. Add 1 piece of fish and about 2 tablespoons Fruit Salsa. *Makes 6 servings*

Fruit Salsa

1 small ripe papaya, peeled, seeded and diced
1 firm small banana, diced
2 green onions, minced
3 tablespoons chopped fresh cilantro or mint
3 tablespoons lime juice
2 jalapeño peppers, seeded and minced*

*Jalapeno peppers can sting and irritate the skin; wear rubber gloves when handling peppers and do not touch eyes. Wash hands after handling.

1. Combine all ingredients in small bowl. Serve at room temperature. *Makes 12 servings*

Seafood Tacos with Fruit Salsa

Oriental Shrimp Burritos

    1 tablespoon vegetable oil
    8 ounces (4 cups packed) shredded cole
        slaw mix with cabbage and carrots
    1 teaspoon bottled minced ginger *or*
        ½ teaspoon dried ginger
    1 teaspoon bottled minced garlic
    1 cup bean sprouts
    ½ cup sliced green onions with tops
    8 (6- or 7-inch) flour tortillas
    10 to 12 ounces cooked peeled medium
        shrimp
    ¼ cup stir-fry sauce
    ¼ teaspoon dried red pepper flakes
        Plum sauce or sweet and sour sauce

1. Heat oil in large, deep skillet over medium-high heat until hot. Add cole slaw mix, ginger and garlic; stir-fry 2 minutes. Add sprouts and onions; stir-fry 3 minutes.

2. While vegetable mixture is cooking, stack tortillas and wrap in wax paper. Microwave on HIGH 1½ minutes or until warm.

3. Add shrimp, stir-fry sauce and pepper flakes to skillet; stir-fry 2 minutes or until heated through. Spoon about ⅓ cup shrimp mixture evenly down center of each tortilla. Fold 1 end of tortilla over filling and roll up. Serve with plum sauce.

Makes 4 servings

Prep and cook time: 10 minutes

Grilled Salmon Quesadillas with Cucumber Salsa

    1 medium cucumber, peeled, seeded and
        finely chopped
    ½ cup green or red salsa
    1 (8-ounce) salmon fillet
    3 tablespoons olive oil, divided
    4 (10-inch) flour tortillas, warmed
    6 ounces goat cheese, crumbled *or* 1½ cups
        (6 ounces) shredded Monterey Jack
        cheese
    ¼ cup drained sliced pickled jalapeño
        peppers

1. Combine cucumber and salsa in small bowl; set aside.

2. Brush salmon with 2 tablespoons oil. Grill, covered, over medium-hot coals 5 to 6 minutes on each side or until fish flakes easily when tested with fork. Transfer to plate; flake with fork.

3. Spoon salmon evenly over half of each tortilla, leaving 1-inch border. Sprinkle with cheese and jalapeño slices. Fold tortillas in half. Brush tortillas with remaining 1 tablespoon oil.

4. Grill quesadillas over medium-hot coals until browned on both sides and cheese is melted. Serve with cucumber salsa.   *Makes 4 servings*

Prep and cook time: 20 minutes

Oriental Shrimp Burritos

Shrimp & Chili Empadas

4 ounces cream cheese, softened
½ cup butter or margarine, softened
¼ cup freshly grated Parmesan cheese
½ teaspoon dried oregano leaves
¼ teaspoon black pepper
1 to 1¼ cups all-purpose flour
Shrimp Filling (recipe follows)
Fresh burnet sprig for garnish

1. Combine cream cheese, butter, Parmesan cheese, oregano and pepper in food processor; process until smooth. Add flour; process until mixture forms dough that leaves side of bowl. Form dough into 2 balls; cover with plastic wrap and refrigerate 30 minutes or until firm.

2. Place 1 ball on lightly floured surface; flatten slightly. Knead dough 5 minutes or until smooth and elastic.

3. Roll dough to ⅛-inch thickness. Cut into circles using 3-inch biscuit cutter. Gather scraps into ball; cover with plastic wrap and refrigerate. Repeat kneading process with second ball. Roll out with reserved scraps to make about 36 rounds total.

4. Preheat oven to 450°F. Prepare Shrimp Filling.

5. To make empadas, place 1 teaspoon filling on each round. Fold in half; seal edges with fork. Place on ungreased baking sheets.

6. Bake empadas 10 minutes or until golden brown. Cool slightly on wire rack; serve warm. Garnish, if desired. *Makes about 36 empadas*

Shrimp Filling

8 ounces cooked, peeled shrimp
1 can (4 ounces) diced green chilies
¼ cup freshly grated Parmesan cheese
2 green onions, chopped
3 to 4 tablespoons chopped fresh cilantro

Process ingredients in food processor until finely chopped. *Makes ¾ cup*

Shrimp & Chili Empadas

Orange Roughy in Parchment Hearts

Parchment paper or foil
4 orange roughy fillets (about 1½ pounds)
Butter
8 ounces fresh asparagus, steamed and
    diagonally cut into 2-inch pieces
1 yellow bell pepper, cut into 16 thin strips
1 red bell pepper, cut into 16 thin strips
1 medium carrot, cut into thin strips
¼ cup dry white wine
3 tablespoons Dijon mustard
2 tablespoons lemon juice
1 teaspoon dried marjoram leaves
¼ teaspoon black pepper

Preheat oven to 375°F. Cut parchment paper into 4 (12-inch) squares. Fold each square in half diagonally and cut into half heart shape. Rinse orange roughy and pat dry with paper towels. Lightly butter inside of each heart. Place 1 piece of fish on 1 side of each heart.

Divide asparagus, bell pepper strips and carrot strips over fish.

Combine wine, mustard, lemon juice, marjoram and black pepper in small bowl. Divide wine mixture over fish.

Fold parchment hearts in half. Beginning at top of heart, fold the edges together, 2 inches at a time. At tip of heart, fold paper up and over.

Place hearts on large baking sheet. Bake 20 to 25 minutes or until fish flakes easily when tested with fork. To serve, cut an "X" through top layer of parchment. *Makes 4 servings*

Salmon en Papillote

⅔ cup FRENCH'S® Dijon Mustard
½ cup (1 stick) butter or margarine, melted
3 cloves garlic, minced
¼ cup minced fresh dill weed *or* 1
    tablespoon dried dill weed
4 pieces (2 pounds) salmon fillet, cut into
    4×3×1½-inch portions
Salt
Ground black pepper
Vegetable cooking spray
2 cups thin vegetable strips, such as bell
    peppers, carrots, leek or celery
2 tablespoons capers, drained

Combine mustard, butter, garlic and dill weed in medium microwave-safe bowl. Cover loosely with vented plastic wrap. Microwave on HIGH 1 minute. Whisk sauce until smooth; set aside.

Sprinkle salmon with salt and black pepper. Cut four 12-inch circles of heavy-duty foil. Coat one side of foil with vegetable cooking spray. Place 1 piece salmon in center of each piece of foil. Spoon about 2 tablespoons mustard sauce over each piece of fish. Reserve remaining sauce. Top fish with vegetables and capers, dividing evenly. Fold foil in half over salmon and vegetables. Seal edges securely with tight double folds.

Place packets on grid. Cook over hot coals 15 to 20 minutes until fish flakes easily with a fork, opening foil packets carefully. Serve with reserved mustard sauce. *Makes 4 servings*

Prep Time: 30 minutes
Cook Time: 20 minutes

*Orange Roughy in
Parchment Heart*

Dazzling
MEATLESS WRAPS

Speedy Garden Roll-Ups

Chick-Pea Spread (recipe follows)
4 (6-inch) flour tortillas
½ cup shredded carrot
½ cup shredded red cabbage
½ cup (2 ounces) shredded reduced-fat
    Cheddar cheese
4 red leaf lettuce leaves

1. Prepare Chick-Pea Spread; set aside.

2. Spread each tortilla with ¼ cup Chick-Pea Spread to about ½ inch from edge. Sprinkle evenly with 2 tablespoons each carrot, cabbage and cheese. Top with 1 lettuce leaf.

3. Roll up tortillas jelly-roll fashion. Seal with additional Chick-Pea Spread.

4. Serve immediately or wrap tightly with plastic wrap and refrigerate up to 4 hours.

Makes 4 servings

Chick-Pea Spread

1 can (about 15 ounces) chick-peas, drained
    and rinsed
¼ cup reduced-fat cream cheese
1 tablespoon finely chopped onion
1 tablespoon chopped cilantro
2 teaspoons lemon juice
2 cloves garlic
½ teaspoon sesame oil
⅛ teaspoon ground black pepper

1. Combine chick-peas, cream cheese, onion, cilantro, lemon juice, garlic, sesame oil and pepper in food processor; process until smooth.

Makes about 1 cup

Speedy Garden Roll-Ups

Mu Shu Vegetables

Peanut Sauce (recipe follows)
3 tablespoons reduced-sodium soy sauce
2 tablespoons dry sherry
1½ tablespoons minced fresh ginger
2 teaspoons cornstarch
1½ teaspoons sesame oil
3 cloves garlic, minced
1 tablespoon peanut oil
3 leeks, washed and cut into 2-inch slivers
3 carrots, peeled and julienned
1 cup thinly sliced fresh shiitake
    mushrooms
1 small head Napa or Savoy cabbage,
    shredded (about 4 cups)
2 cups mung bean sprouts, rinsed and
    drained
8 ounces firm tofu, drained and cut into
    2½×¼-inch strips
12 (8-inch) flour tortillas, warmed*
¾ cup finely chopped honey roasted peanuts

*Tortillas can be softened and warmed in microwave oven just before using. Stack tortillas and wrap in plastic wrap. Microwave on HIGH ½ to 1 minute, turning over and rotating ¼ turn once during heating.

Prepare Peanut Sauce; set aside. Combine soy sauce, sherry, ginger, cornstarch, sesame oil and garlic in small bowl until smooth; set aside.

Heat wok over medium-high heat 1 minute or until hot. Drizzle peanut oil into wok and heat 30 seconds. Add leeks, carrots and mushrooms; stir-fry 2 minutes. Add cabbage; stir-fry 3 minutes or until just tender. Add bean sprouts and tofu; stir-fry 1 minute or until hot. Stir soy sauce mixture and add to wok. Cook and stir 1 minute or until thickened.

Spread each tortilla with about 1 teaspoon Peanut Sauce. Spoon ½ cup vegetable mixture on bottom half of tortilla; sprinkle with 1 tablespoon peanuts.

Fold bottom edge of tortilla over filling; fold in side edges. Roll up to completely enclose filling. Or, spoon ½ cup vegetable mixture on one half of tortilla. Fold bottom edge over filling. Fold in one side edge. Serve with Peanut Sauce.

Makes 6 servings

Peanut Sauce

3 tablespoons sugar
3 tablespoons dry sherry
3 tablespoons reduced-sodium soy sauce
3 tablespoons water
2 teaspoons white wine vinegar
⅓ cup creamy peanut butter

Combine all ingredients except peanut butter in small saucepan. Bring to a boil over medium-high heat, stirring constantly. Boil 1 minute or until sugar melts. Stir in peanut butter until smooth; cool to room temperature.

Makes ⅔ cup

Eggplant Crêpes with Roasted Tomato Sauce

Roasted Tomato Sauce (recipe follows)
2 eggplants (about 8 to 9 inches long)
Nonstick olive oil cooking spray
1 package (10 ounces) frozen chopped
    spinach, thawed and pressed dry
1 cup ricotta cheese
½ cup grated Parmesan cheese
1¼ cups (5 ounces) shredded Gruyère*
    cheese
Fresh oregano leaves for garnish

*Gruyère cheese is a Swiss cheese that has been aged for 10 to 12 months. Any Swiss cheese may be substituted.

Prepare Roasted Tomato Sauce; set aside. *Reduce oven temperature to 425°F.*

Cut eggplants lengthwise into ¼-inch-thick slices. Arrange 18 of largest slices on nonstick baking sheets in single layer. Spray both sides of eggplant slices with cooking spray. (Reserve any remaining slices for other uses.) Bake eggplant 10 minutes; turn and bake 5 to 10 minutes more or until tender. Cool. *Reduce oven temperature to 350°F.*

Combine spinach, ricotta and Parmesan cheese; mix well. Spray 12×8-inch baking pan with cooking spray. Spread spinach mixture evenly on eggplant slices; roll up slices, beginning at short ends. Place rolls, seam side down, in baking dish. Cover dish with foil and bake 25 minutes. Uncover; sprinkle rolls with Gruyère cheese. Bake, uncovered, 5 minutes more or until cheese is melted. Serve with Roasted Tomato Sauce. Garnish, if desired.   *Makes 4 to 6 servings*

Roasted Tomato Sauce

20 ripe plum tomatoes (about 2⅔ pounds),
    cut in half and seeded
3 tablespoons olive oil, divided
½ teaspoon salt
⅓ cup minced fresh basil
½ teaspoon ground black pepper

Preheat oven to 450°F. Toss tomatoes with 1 tablespoon oil and salt. Place, cut sides down, on nonstick baking sheet. Bake 20 to 25 minutes or until skins are blistered. Cool. Process tomatoes, remaining 2 tablespoons oil, basil and pepper in food processor until smooth.

Makes about 1 cup

*Eggplant Crêpes with
Roasted Tomato Sauce*

Vegetable & Pesto Salad Pita Wraps

¼ cup mayonnaise
¼ cup refrigerated pesto sauce
4 cups assorted fresh vegetables, such as shredded carrots, onion strips, sliced radishes, cubed zucchini and bell peppers
4 pita breads
4 leaves leaf lettuce
4 slices provolone cheese
Chopped tomato

1. In medium bowl, combine mayonnaise and pesto; mix well.

2. Add vegetables; toss to coat.

3. Wrap two pita breads in paper towels. Microwave at HIGH 20 to 30 seconds or just until warm. Repeat with remaining pita breads. Top half of each pita bread with 1 lettuce leaf, 1 slice cheese and ¼ of vegetable mixture. Sprinkle with tomato. Fold other half of pita bread over vegetables. *Makes 4 servings*

Low-Fat Chimichangas

1 (16-ounce) can black beans, rinsed and drained
1 (8-ounce) can stewed tomatoes
2 to 3 teaspoons chili powder
1 teaspoon dried oregano
22 to 24 (6-inch) corn tortillas
1 cup finely chopped green onions including tops
1½ cups (6 ounces) shredded JARLSBERG LITE™ Cheese

Mix beans, tomatoes, chili powder and oregano in medium saucepan. Cover and simmer 5 minutes. Uncover and simmer, stirring and crushing some of beans with wooden spoon, 5 minutes longer. Set aside. Warm tortillas according to package directions; keep warm. Place one tablespoon bean mixture on center of each tortilla. Sprinkle with rounded teaspoon onion, then rounded tablespoon cheese. Fold opposite sides of tortillas over mixture, forming square packets. Place folded sides down on nonstick skillet. Repeat until all ingredients are used. Cook, covered, over low heat 3 to 5 minutes until heated through and bottoms are crispy. Serve at once or keep warm on covered warming tray. *Makes 6 to 8 servings*

Vegetable & Pesto Salad Pita Wrap

Gourmet Bean & Spinach Burritos

Avocado Relish (recipe follows)
1 pound spinach, divided
2 teaspoons olive oil
1 cup finely chopped onion
2 cloves garlic, minced
2 cans (15 ounces each) black beans, drained
1 can (10 ounces) whole tomatoes with green chilies, undrained
2 teaspoons ground cumin
½ teaspoon ground oregano
8 (8-inch) flour tortillas
2 cups (8 ounces) shredded Monterey Jack cheese
Sour cream (optional)

1. Prepare Avocado Relish.

2. Wash and dry spinach. Remove stems from spinach leaves; discard stems. Set aside 24 to 30 large leaves. Stack remaining leaves and cut crosswise into ¼-inch-wide pieces. Set aside.

3. Heat olive oil in large nonstick skillet over medium heat until hot. Add onion and garlic; cook and stir 5 minutes or until tender. Add beans, tomatoes, cumin and oregano. Simmer, uncovered, until mixture is dry. Remove from heat; mash bean mixture with potato masher.

4. Preheat oven to 350°F. Arrange 3 to 4 whole spinach leaves on each tortilla. Spoon bean mixture onto bottom half of tortillas; sprinkle cheese evenly over bean mixture.

5. Roll up to enclose filling. Repeat with remaining tortillas, spinach and bean mixture.

6. Arrange, seam side down, in 12×8-inch baking dish. Cover with foil. Bake 20 minutes or until heated through.

7. To serve, arrange about ½ cup spinach pieces on each serving plate; top with 2 burritos. Serve with Avocado Relish. Garnish, if desired.

Makes 4 servings

Avocado Relish

1 large, firm ripe avocado, finely diced
2 tablespoons fresh lime juice
¾ cup finely chopped, seeded tomato
½ cup minced green onions
⅓ cup minced fresh cilantro
½ to 1 teaspoon hot pepper sauce

1. Combine avocado and lime juice in bowl; toss. Add tomato, onions, cilantro and hot sauce; toss gently. Cover and refrigerate 1 hour. Serve at room temperature.   *Makes about 2¼ cups*

Spinach and Mushroom Enchiladas

2 packages (10 ounces each) frozen chopped spinach, thawed and well drained
1 can (15 ounces) pinto beans, rinsed and drained
1½ cups sliced mushrooms
3 teaspoons chili powder, divided
¼ teaspoon red pepper flakes
1 can (8 ounces) low-sodium tomato sauce
2 tablespoons water
½ teaspoon hot pepper sauce
8 (8-inch) corn tortillas
1 cup (4 ounces) shredded Monterey Jack cheese

1. Combine spinach, beans, mushrooms, 2 teaspoons chili powder and red pepper flakes in large skillet over medium heat. Cook and stir 5 minutes; remove from heat.

2. Combine tomato sauce, water, remaining 1 teaspoon chili powder and pepper sauce in medium skillet. Dip tortillas into tomato sauce mixture; stack tortillas on waxed paper.

3. Divide spinach filling into 8 portions. Spoon onto centers of tortillas; roll up and place in 12×8-inch microwavable dish. (Secure rolls with toothpicks if desired.) Spread remaining tomato sauce mixture over enchiladas.

4. Cover with vented plastic wrap. Microwave at MEDIUM (50%) 10 minutes or until heated through. Sprinkle with cheese. Microwave at MEDIUM 3 minutes or until cheese is melted. Serve with shredded lettuce and chopped tomatoes, if desired. *Makes 4 servings*

Pinto Bean & Zucchini Burritos

6 flour tortillas (6 inches each)
¾ cup GUILTLESS GOURMET® Pinto Bean Dip (spicy)
2 teaspoons water
1 teaspoon olive oil
1 medium zucchini, chopped
¼ cup chopped green onions
¼ cup GUILTLESS GOURMET® Green Tomatillo Salsa
1 cup GUILTLESS GOURMET® Salsa (medium), divided
1½ cups shredded lettuce
Fresh cilantro leaves (optional)

Preheat oven to 300°F. Wrap tortillas in foil. Bake 10 minutes or until softened and heated through. Meanwhile, combine bean dip and water in small bowl. Heat oil in large skillet over medium-high heat until hot. Add zucchini and onions. Cook and stir until zucchini is crisp-tender; stir in bean dip mixture and tomatillo salsa.

Fill each tortilla with zucchini mixture, dividing evenly. Roll up tortillas; place on 6 individual serving plates. Top with salsa. Serve hot with lettuce. Garnish with cilantro, if desired.
Makes 6 servings

Confetti Cheese Rotolo with Seasoned Eggplant

8 lasagna noodles
2 tablespoons olive oil
1 cup fresh or frozen corn kernels
1 cup coarsely chopped mushrooms
½ cup sliced green onions and tops
½ cup chopped carrot
1 medium red bell pepper, diced
2 cloves garlic, minced
1 teaspoon dried basil leaves
1 cup ricotta cheese
¾ cup (3 ounces) shredded mozzarella
    cheese
½ cup grated Parmesan cheese
1 egg
½ teaspoon salt
½ teaspoon ground black pepper
    Seasoned Eggplant (recipe follows)

1. Cook lasagna noodles according to package directions until al dente. Drain in colander. Set aside.

2. Heat oil in large skillet over medium heat until hot. Add corn, mushrooms, onions, carrot, bell pepper, garlic and basil; cook and stir 8 minutes or until tender. Cool.

3. Process cheeses, egg, salt and black pepper in food processor until smooth; add vegetables and process using on/off pulsing action until vegetables are finely chopped.

4. Preheat oven to 350°F. Spread about ½ cup cheese mixture on each noodle; roll up. Place, seam side down, in 11×7-inch baking pan. Repeat with remaining noodles and cheese mixture.

5. Loosely cover pan with foil. Bake rotolo 35 to 40 minutes or until heated through.

6. Meanwhile prepare Seasoned Eggplant.

7. Remove rotolo from oven and let stand 5 to 10 minutes. Cut each rotolo into halves, if desired. Serve with Seasoned Eggplant.
Makes 8 servings

Seasoned Eggplant

1 tablespoon olive oil
1 medium eggplant, cubed (1 pound)
1 cup chopped onions
6 cloves garlic, minced
¾ cup canned vegetable broth
½ cup minced parsley
2 teaspoons sugar
¾ teaspoon dried basil leaves
¾ teaspoon dried tarragon leaves
½ teaspoon salt
¼ teaspoon ground black pepper

1. Heat oil in large skillet over medium heat until hot. Add eggplant, onions and garlic; cook and stir 10 minutes or until vegetables are tender.

2. Add remaining ingredients; cook, covered, over medium heat 15 to 20 minutes or until liquid is absorbed.   *Makes about 3 cups*

*Confetti Cheese Rotolo with
Seasoned Eggplant*

Miami Rice and Bean Burritos

1 medium packaged cored fresh pineapple
2 tablespoons olive oil, divided
1 cup chopped seeded tomatoes
2 tablespoons light brown sugar
⅓ cup chopped fresh cilantro
3 tablespoons balsamic vinegar, divided
1 cup canned chicken broth
⅔ cup prepared mild or hot salsa
¾ cup uncooked long-grain white rice
2 cloves garlic, minced
1½ teaspoons ground cumin
½ teaspoon ground allspice
1 can (16 ounces) pinto beans, rinsed and
   drained
8 (7-inch) flour tortillas
   Sour cream
   Sliced green onions

1. Preheat oven to 400°F.

2. Cut pineapple lengthwise in half with chef's knife. Coarsely chop pineapple.

3. Toss pineapple and 1 tablespoon oil on large nonstick baking sheet. Bake 20 minutes or until lightly browned, stirring halfway through baking time. Turn oven off.

4. Transfer pineapple to large bowl; stir in tomatoes and brown sugar. Let cool to room temperature. Stir in cilantro and 1 tablespoon vinegar.

5. Bring chicken broth and salsa to a boil in heavy, medium saucepan over high heat. Stir in rice. Reduce heat to low; simmer, covered, 20 minutes or until rice is tender and liquid is absorbed.

6. Heat remaining 1 tablespoon oil in large saucepan over medium heat. Add garlic, cumin and allspice; cook and stir 3 minutes. Add beans and remaining 2 tablespoons vinegar; cook and stir 2 minutes or until heated through.

7. Coarsely mash bean mixture with potato masher.

8. Preheat oven to 350°F. Spread about 3 tablespoons bean mixture evenly on bottom half of 1 tortilla; top with rice mixture.

9. To form, fold right edge of tortilla up over filling; fold bottom edge over filling, then loosely roll up, leaving left end of burrito open. Repeat with remaining tortillas, bean mixture and rice mixture.

10. Place burritos in ungreased 12×8×2-inch baking dish. Cover; bake 20 minutes or until heated through. Serve with pineapple salsa, sour cream and sliced green onions. Garnish as desired.

Makes 4 servings

Veggie Pita Wraps

½ cup reduced-fat mayonnaise
1 clove garlic, minced
¼ teaspoon dried marjoram leaves
¼ teaspoon dried tarragon leaves
4 whole wheat pita breads
4 slices Cheddar cheese
½ cup rinsed and drained alfalfa sprouts
½ cucumber, thinly sliced
8 tomato slices
1 medium red onion, thinly sliced
2 cups chopped romaine lettuce

1. Combine mayonnaise, garlic, marjoram and tarragon in small bowl.

2. Wrap 2 pita breads in paper towels. Microwave at High 20 to 30 seconds or just until soft and slightly warm. Repeat with remaining pita breads.

3. Spread 2 tablespoons mayonnaise mixture over each pita bread. Fold pita breads in half; divide cheese, alfalfa sprouts, cucumber, tomato, onion and lettuce among breads.   *Makes 4 servings*

Grilled Portobello & Pepper Wraps

1 container (8 ounces) sour cream
1 teaspoon dried dill weed
1 teaspoon onion powder
2 tablespoons vegetable oil
1 large clove garlic, minced
2 portobello mushrooms, stems removed
1 large green bell pepper, quartered
1 large red bell pepper, quartered
6 (6-inch) flour tortillas, warmed

1. Prepare barbecue grill for direct cooking.

2. Combine sour cream, dill and onion powder in small bowl; set aside. Combine oil and garlic in another small bowl; set aside.

3. Spray barbecue grid with nonstick cooking spray. Place mushrooms and bell peppers on prepared grid. Brush lightly with oil mixture; season with salt and black pepper to taste.

4. Grill, on covered grill, over medium-hot coals 10 minutes or until bell peppers are crisp-tender, turning halfway through grilling time. Remove mushrooms and peppers to cutting board; cut into 1-inch slices.

5. Place on serving platter. Serve with sour cream mixture and tortillas.   *Makes 4 to 6 servings*

Serving Suggestion: Serve with spicy refried beans and salsa.

Prep and Cook Time: 18 minutes

Veggie Pita Wrap

Bean and Vegetable Burritos

1 tablespoon olive oil
1 medium onion, thinly sliced
1 jalapeño pepper,* seeded, minced
1 tablespoon chili powder
3 cloves garlic, minced
2 teaspoons dried oregano leaves
1 teaspoon ground cumin
1 large sweet potato, baked, cooled, peeled and diced
1 can black beans or pinto beans, drained and rinsed
1 cup frozen whole kernel corn, thawed and drained
1 green bell pepper, chopped
2 tablespoons lime juice
¾ cup (3 ounces) shredded reduced-fat Monterey Jack cheese
4 flour tortillas (10-inch)
Sour cream (optional)

* Jalapeño peppers can sting and irritate the skin; wear rubber gloves when handling and do not touch eyes. Wash hands after handling.

Preheat oven to 350°F. Heat oil over medium heat in large saucepan. Add onion; cook and stir 10 minutes or until golden. Add jalapeño pepper, chili powder, garlic, oregano and cumin; stir 1 minute more. Add 1 tablespoon water and stir; remove from heat. Stir in sweet potato, beans, corn, bell pepper and lime juice.

Spoon 2 tablespoons cheese in center of each tortilla. Top with 1 cup filling. Fold all 4 sides around filling to enclose. Place burritos seam side down on baking sheet. Cover with foil and bake 30 minutes or until heated through. Serve with sour cream, if desired. *Makes 4 servings*

Vegetable Calzone

1 loaf (1 pound) frozen bread dough
1 package (10 ounces) frozen chopped broccoli, thawed and well drained
1 cup (8 ounces) SARGENTO® Light Ricotta Cheese
1 cup (4 ounces) SARGENTO® Classic Shredded Mozzarella Cheese
1 clove garlic, minced
¼ teaspoon white pepper
1 egg beaten with 1 tablespoon water
1 jar (16 ounces) spaghetti sauce, heated (optional)
SARGENTO® Grated Parmesan Cheese (optional)

Thaw bread dough; let rise according to package directions. Combine broccoli, Ricotta and Mozzarella cheeses, garlic and pepper. Punch down bread dough; turn out onto lightly floured surface. Divide into 4 equal pieces. One at a time, roll out each piece into 8-inch circle. Place about ¼ cup cheese mixture on half of circle, leaving 1-inch border. Fold dough over to cover filling, forming semi-circle; press and crimp edges with fork tines to seal. Brush with egg mixture. Place on greased baking sheet; bake at 350°F 30 minutes or until brown and puffed. Transfer to rack; cool 10 minutes. Top with hot spaghetti sauce and Parmesan cheese. *Makes 4 servings*

Bean and Vegetable Burrito

Cabbage-Cheese Strudel

    1 tablespoon vegetable oil
    1 cup chopped onions
    ½ cup sliced leeks
    ½ cup sliced button mushrooms
    ½ cup seeded and chopped tomato
    ¼ head green cabbage, shredded
    1 cup broccoli florets, steamed
 1½ teaspoons caraway seeds, crushed, divided
    1 teaspoon dried dill weed
    ½ teaspoon salt
    ¼ teaspoon ground black pepper
    1 package (8 ounces) cream cheese,
        softened
    1 egg, beaten
    ¾ cup cooked brown rice
    ¾ cup (3 ounces) shredded Cheddar cheese
    6 sheets frozen phyllo pastry, thawed
    6 to 8 tablespoons margarine or butter,
        melted

Heat oil in large saucepan over medium heat until hot. Add onions and leeks; cook and stir 3 minutes. Add mushrooms and tomato; cook and stir 5 minutes. Add cabbage, broccoli, 1 teaspoon caraway seeds, dill weed, salt and pepper. Cover; cook over medium heat 8 to 10 minutes or until cabbage wilts. Remove cover; cook 10 minutes more or until cabbage is soft and beginning to brown.

Combine cream cheese, egg, rice and Cheddar cheese in medium bowl. Stir into cabbage mixture until blended.

Preheat oven to 375°F. Unroll phyllo dough. Cover with plastic wrap and damp, clean kitchen towel. Brush 1 phyllo dough sheet with margarine. Top with 2 more sheets, brushing each with margarine. Spoon half of cabbage mixture 2 inches from short end of phyllo. Spread mixture to cover about half of phyllo. Roll up dough from short end with filling. Place, seam side down, on greased cookie sheet. Flatten roll slightly with hands and brush with margarine. Repeat with remaining phyllo, margarine and cabbage mixture. Sprinkle tops of rolls with remaining ½ teaspoon caraway seeds.

Bake 45 to 50 minutes or until golden brown. Cool 10 minutes. Cut each roll diagonally into 3 pieces with serrated knife.   *Makes 6 servings*

Primavera Strudel

4½ teaspoons olive oil
1 small onion, chopped
2 cloves garlic, minced
8 ounces thin asparagus, cut diagonally into
    ¾-inch pieces
1 red bell pepper, cut into julienne strips
1 cup frozen peas, thawed
½ teaspoon salt
½ teaspoon black pepper
1 container (15 ounces) ricotta cheese
¾ cup grated Asiago cheese
⅓ cup chopped fresh basil
1 egg, lightly beaten
10 frozen phyllo dough sheets, thawed
½ cup butter, melted
6 tablespoons dry bread crumbs, divided

1. Heat oil in large skillet over medium heat. Add onion and garlic; cook and stir 5 minutes. Add asparagus and bell pepper; cook and stir 6 to 7 minutes or until crisp-tender. Stir in peas, salt and black pepper. Remove from heat; let cool to room temperature.

2. Preheat oven to 375°F. Combine ricotta, Asiago, basil and egg in large bowl; mix well. Stir in vegetable mixture.

3. Line 15×10-inch jelly-roll pan with foil; set aside.

4. Place 1 sheet phyllo on work surface. (Keep remaining phyllo covered with plastic wrap and damp towel to keep from drying out.) Lightly brush phyllo with butter. Top with second phyllo sheet. Lightly brush with butter and sprinkle with 1 tablespoon bread crumbs. Place third phyllo sheet over crumbs; lightly brush with butter; sprinkle with 1 tablespoon bread crumbs. Top with fourth phyllo sheet and 1 tablespoon bread crumbs. Place fifth phyllo sheet over bread crumbs and brush with butter.

5. Spoon ½ of ricotta mixture along 1 short side of phyllo in 3-inch-wide strip, beginning 1½ inches in from short side and leaving 2-inch border on long sides. Fold long sides in over filling; lightly brush folded edges with butter. Starting at filled side, gently roll up, jelly-roll style, forming strudel. Lightly brush strudel with butter. Transfer to prepared pan, seam side down.

6. Repeat process with remaining ingredients to make second strudel. Bake strudels 25 to 28 minutes or until golden brown. Cool 10 minutes before slicing. Serve warm.   *Makes 8 servings*

Veggie Calzones

1½ cups BIRDS EYE® frozen Farm Fresh
    Mixtures Broccoli, Red Peppers,
    Onions & Mushrooms
½ cup ricotta cheese
½ cup shredded mozzarella cheese
¼ cup grated Parmesan cheese
1 teaspoon dried Italian seasoning
¼ teaspoon pepper
1 pound fresh pizza dough or thawed frozen
    bread dough
1 egg, beaten

- Preheat oven to 425°F.

- Rinse vegetables under warm water to thaw; drain well and pat gently with paper towel.

- In medium bowl, combine vegetables, cheeses, Italian seasoning and pepper.

- Divide dough into 4 pieces. Roll out each piece into 6-inch circle.* Spoon ¼ of vegetable mixture over ½ of each circle, leaving ½-inch border. Moisten edge of dough with water; fold dough over filling to form half circle. Pinch edges well to seal. Cut several slits in top of dough; brush with egg.

- Place on greased baking sheet and bake 12 to 14 minutes or until golden brown.

Makes 4 servings

*Dough is easier to work with on nonfloured surface.

Prep Time: 10 minutes
Cook Time: 15 minutes

Spicy Empanadas

1 can (8¾ ounces) garbanzo beans, drained
1 teaspoon vegetable oil
¼ cup minced fresh onion
2 tablespoons minced green bell pepper
¼ teaspoon LAWRY'S® Garlic Powder with
    Parsley
2 tablespoons currants
2 tablespoons chopped pitted black olives
1 package (1 ounce) LAWRY'S® Taco
    Spices & Seasonings
1 teaspoon lemon juice
¼ cup (1 ounce) shredded Monterey Jack
    cheese
    All-purpose flour
1 sheet frozen puff pastry, thawed
1 egg yolk, beaten

In food processor or blender, place garbanzo beans. Pulse 30 seconds to chop finely; set aside. In large skillet, heat oil. Add onion, bell pepper and Garlic Powder with Parsley; cook over medium-high heat 3 to 4 minutes or until vegetables are crisp-tender. Add beans, currants, olives, Taco Spices & Seasonings and lemon juice; cook until mixture thickens, stirring occasionally. Remove from heat; stir in cheese. On lightly floured surface, roll out pastry sheet to approximately 18×10-inch rectangle; cut out six to eight (4-inch) circles. Spoon equal amounts of filling onto half of each circle; fold pastry over to form half circle. Press edges together with fork to seal. Place empanadas on greased baking sheet; brush with egg yolk. Bake 18 to 20 minutes or until golden brown.   *Makes 6 to 8 empanadas*

Veggie Calzone

Glorious BRUNCH FAVORITES

French Breakfast Crêpes

   1 cup all-purpose flour
   1 cup skim milk
   ⅔ cup EGG BEATERS® Healthy Real Egg
      Substitute
   1 tablespoon FLEISCHMANN'S® Original
      Spread (70% Corn Oil), melted

In medium bowl, combine flour, milk, Egg Beaters® and spread; let stand 30 minutes.

Heat lightly greased 8-inch nonstick skillet or crêpe pan over medium-high heat. Pour in scant ¼ cup batter, tilting pan to cover bottom. Cook for 1 to 2 minutes; turn and cook for 30 seconds to 1 minute more. Place on waxed paper. Stir batter and repeat to make 10 crêpes. Fill with desired fillings or use in recipes calling for prepared crêpes.   *Makes 10 crêpes*

Strawberry Yogurt Crêpes: In medium bowl, combine 1 pint low-fat vanilla yogurt and 2 tablespoons orange-flavored liqueur or orange juice; reserve ½ cup. Stir 2 cups sliced strawberries into remaining yogurt mixture. Spoon ¼ cup strawberry mixture down center of each prepared crêpe; roll up. Top with reserved yogurt mixture.

Blueberry Crêpes: In medium saucepan, combine 2 cups fresh or frozen blueberries, ⅓ cup water, 2 teaspoons lemon juice and 2 teaspoons cornstarch. Cook over medium-high heat, stirring frequently until mixture thickens and begins to boil. Reduce heat; simmer 1 minute. Chill. Spoon 2 tablespoons low-fat vanilla yogurt down center of each prepared crêpe; roll up. Top with blueberry sauce.

Prep Time: 10 minutes
Cook Time: 40 minutes

Strawberry Yogurt Crêpe

Scrambled Egg Burritos

Nonstick cooking spray
1 red bell pepper, chopped
5 green onions, sliced
½ teaspoon red pepper flakes
1 cup cholesterol-free egg substitute
1 tablespoon chopped fresh cilantro or parsley
4 (8-inch) flour tortillas
½ cup (2 ounces) shredded, reduced-fat Monterey Jack cheese
⅓ cup salsa

1. Spray medium nonstick skillet with cooking spray. Heat over medium heat until hot. Add bell pepper, green onions and red pepper flakes. Cook and stir 3 minutes or until vegetables are crisp-tender.

2. Add egg substitute to vegetables. Reduce heat to low. Cook and stir 3 minutes or until set. Sprinkle with cilantro.

3. Stack tortillas and wrap in paper towels. Microwave at HIGH 1 minute or until tortillas are hot.

4. Divide egg mixture among tortillas. Sprinkle with cheese. Fold sides over to enclose filling. Serve with salsa.   *Makes 4 servings*

Ready to serve in 18 minutes.

Note: Five beaten large eggs can be substituted for the cholesterol-free egg substitute, if desired.

Breakfast Burritos with Tomato-Basil Topping

1 large tomato, diced
2 teaspoons finely chopped basil *or* ½ teaspoon dried basil leaves
1 medium potato, peeled and shredded (about 1 cup)
¼ cup chopped onion
2 teaspoons FLEISCHMANN'S® Original Spread (70% Corn Oil)
1 cup EGG BEATERS® Healthy Real Egg Substitute
⅛ teaspoon ground black pepper
4 (8-inch) flour tortillas, warmed
⅓ cup shredded reduced-fat Cheddar cheese

In small bowl, combine tomato and basil; set aside.

In large nonstick skillet, over medium heat, sauté potato and onion in spread until tender. Pour Egg Beaters® into skillet; sprinkle with pepper. Cook, stirring occasionally until mixture is set.

Divide egg mixture evenly between tortillas; top with cheese. Fold tortillas over egg mixture. Top with tomato mixture.   *Makes 4 servings*

Prep Time: 15 minutes
Cook Time: 25 minutes

Scrambled Egg Burrito

Fancy Swiss Omelet Roll

6 eggs
1 cup milk
½ cup all-purpose flour
2 tablespoons butter or margarine, melted
½ teaspoon salt
¼ teaspoon white pepper
½ cup chopped roasted red pepper
2 ounces prosciutto or ham, thinly sliced
    and cut into strips
1 cup (4 ounces) shredded Swiss cheese
2 tablespoons chopped fresh basil

1. Preheat oven to 350°F. Line bottom and sides of 15×10-inch jelly-roll pan with foil. Generously spray bottom and sides of foil with nonstick cooking spray.

2. Combine eggs, milk, flour, butter, salt and white pepper in medium bowl. Beat with electric mixer at medium speed until well blended. Pour into prepared pan. Bake 10 minutes. Sprinkle with red pepper and prosciutto.

3. Continue baking 8 to 10 minutes or until eggs are set, but not dry. Immediately sprinkle with cheese and basil.

4. Beginning with short end of omelet, carefully roll up omelet, using foil to gently lift omelet from pan.

5. To serve, transfer omelet roll to serving platter and cut into 1¼-inch-thick slices.

Makes 4 servings

Hawaiian Breakfast Wrap

6 eggs
¼ cup milk or water
¼ cup chopped ham
¼ cup chopped DOLE® Red or Green Bell
    Pepper
2 tablespoons margarine
1 can (8 ounces) DOLE Crushed Pineapple,
    drained
4 (8-inch) flour tortillas

• Beat together eggs and milk in medium bowl, until blended. Set aside.

• Cook ham and bell pepper in hot margarine over medium heat in large skillet, until ham is lightly browned and vegetables are tender-crisp. Stir in egg mixture and pineapple. Scramble until desired doneness, stirring constantly.

• Evenly divide egg mixture onto flour tortillas. Roll sides up. Serve with watermelon wedges and lime slice, if desired. Serve immediately.

Makes 4 servings

Prep Time: 15 minutes

Fancy Swiss Omelet Roll

Ham and Egg Enchiladas

2 tablespoons butter or margarine
1 small red bell pepper, chopped
3 green onions with tops, sliced
½ cup diced ham
8 eggs
8 (7- to 8-inch) flour tortillas
2 cups (8 ounces) shredded Colby-Jack
   cheese or Monterey Jack cheese with
   jalapeño peppers, divided
1 can (10 ounces) enchilada sauce
½ cup prepared salsa
   Sliced avocado, fresh cilantro and red
   pepper slices for garnish

1. Preheat oven to 350°F.

2. Melt butter in large nonstick skillet over medium heat. Add bell pepper and onions; cook and stir 2 minutes. Add ham; cook and stir 1 minute.

3. Lightly beat eggs with wire whisk in medium bowl. Add eggs to skillet; cook until eggs are set, but still soft, stirring occasionally.

4. Spoon about ⅓ cup egg mixture evenly down center of each tortilla; top with 1 tablespoon cheese. Roll tortillas up and place, seam side down, in shallow 11×7-inch baking dish.

5. Combine enchilada sauce and salsa in small bowl; pour evenly over enchiladas.

6. Cover enchiladas with foil; bake 20 minutes. Uncover; sprinkle with remaining cheese. Continue baking 10 minutes or until enchiladas are hot and cheese is melted. Garnish, if desired. Serve immediately.   *Makes 4 servings*

Brunch Rice

1 teaspoon margarine
¾ cup shredded carrots
¾ cup diced green bell pepper
¾ cup (about 3 ounces) sliced mushrooms
6 egg whites, beaten
2 eggs, beaten
½ cup skim milk
½ teaspoon salt
¼ teaspoon ground black pepper
3 cups cooked brown rice
½ cup (2 ounces) shredded Cheddar cheese
6 corn tortillas, warmed

Heat margarine in large skillet over medium-high heat until hot. Add carrots, bell pepper and mushrooms; cook and stir 2 minutes. Combine egg whites, eggs, milk, salt and black pepper in small bowl. Reduce heat to medium and pour egg mixture over vegetables. Continue stirring 1½ to 2 minutes. Add rice and cheese; stir to gently separate grains. Heat 2 minutes. Spoon mixture into warmed corn tortillas; roll up to enclose filling.   *Makes 6 servings*

Microwave Directions: Heat margarine in 2- to 3-quart microproof baking dish. Add carrots, bell pepper and mushrooms; cover and cook on HIGH 4 minutes. Combine egg whites, eggs, milk, salt and black pepper in small bowl; pour over vegetables. Cook on HIGH 4 minutes, stirring with fork after each minute to cut cooked eggs into small pieces. Stir in rice and cheese; cook on HIGH about 1 minute or until hot. Spoon mixture into warmed corn tortillas.

Favorite recipe from **USA Rice Federation**

Ham and Egg Enchiladas

Breakfast Burritos with Baked Citrus Fruit

4 green onions, thinly sliced, divided
1¼ cups egg substitute
2 tablespoons diced mild green chilies
½ cup (2 ounces) shredded reduced-fat Monterey Jack or Cheddar cheese
¼ cup lightly packed fresh cilantro
4 (7-inch) flour tortillas
¼ cup salsa
¼ cup low-fat sour cream
Baked Citrus Fruit (recipe follows)

Spray large nonstick skillet with cooking spray. Heat over medium heat. Set aside ¼ cup green onions. Add remaining onions, egg substitute and chilies to skillet. Cook, stirring occasionally, about 4 minutes or until eggs are softly set. Stir in cheese and cilantro. Continue cooking, folding egg mixture over until cooked to desired doneness, about 1 minute.

Stack tortillas and wrap in paper towels. Microwave at HIGH about 1 minute or until hot. Divivde eggs among tortillas. Fold sides over filling to enclose. Place burritos seam side down on plates. Top each with salsa, 1 tablespoon sour cream and reserved green onions. Serve with Baked Citrus Fruit. *Makes 4 servings*

Baked Citrus Fruit

2 oranges, peeled and sliced
1 grapefruit, peeled and sliced
1½ tablespoons lightly packed brown sugar
½ teaspoon ground cinnamon

Preheat oven to 400°F. Divide fruit slices into 4 portions. Arrange each portion on baking sheet, overlapping slices. Combine brown sugar and cinnamon in small bowl. Sprinkle 1 teaspoon brown sugar mixture over each serving of fruit. Bake 5 minutes or until fruit is hot.

Makes 4 servings

Spinach Cheese Roulade

4 teaspoons FLEISCHMANN'S® Original Spread (70% Corn Oil), divided
2 tablespoons all-purpose flour
1 cup skim milk
2 cups EGG BEATERS® Healthy Real Egg Substitute
1 medium onion, chopped
1 (10-ounce) package fresh spinach, coarsely chopped
½ cup low-fat cottage cheese (1% milkfat)
1 (8-ounce) can no-salt-added tomato sauce
½ teaspoon dried basil leaves
½ teaspoon garlic powder

In small saucepan, over medium heat, melt 3 teaspoons spread; blend in flour. Cook, stirring until smooth and bubbly; remove from heat. Gradually blend in milk; return to heat. Heat to a boil, stirring constantly until thickened; cool slightly. Stir in Egg Beaters®. Spread mixture in bottom of 15½×10½×1-inch baking pan that has been greased, lined with foil and greased again. Bake at 350°F for 20 minutes or until set.

In medium skillet, sauté onion in remaining 1 teaspoon spread until tender. Add spinach and cook until wilted, about 3 minutes; stir in cottage cheese. Keep warm.

Invert egg mixture onto large piece of foil. Spread with spinach mixture; roll up from short end. In small saucepan, combine tomato sauce, basil and garlic powder; heat until warm. To serve, slice roll into 8 pieces; top with warm sauce. *Makes 8 servings*

Prep Time: 30 minutes

Cook Time: 25 minutes

Mexican Omelet Roll-Ups with Avocado Sauce

>   8 eggs
>   2 tablespoons milk
>   1 tablespoon margarine or butter
> 1½ cups (6 ounces) shredded Monterey Jack
>   cheese
>   1 large tomato, seeded and chopped
>   ¼ cup chopped fresh cilantro
>   8 (7-inch) corn tortillas
> 1½ cups salsa
>   2 medium avocados, chopped
>   ¼ cup reduced-fat sour cream
>   2 tablespoons diced green chiles
>   1 tablespoon fresh lemon juice
>   1 teaspoon hot pepper sauce
>   ¼ teaspoon salt

PREHEAT oven to 350°F. Spray 13×9-inch baking dish with nonstick cooking spray.

WHISK eggs and milk in medium bowl until blended. Melt margarine in large skillet over medium heat; add egg mixture to skillet. Cook and stir 5 minutes or until eggs are set, but still soft. Remove from heat. Stir in cheese, tomato and cilantro.

SPOON about ⅓ cup egg mixture evenly down center of each tortilla. Roll up tortillas and place, seam side down, in prepared dish. Pour salsa evenly over tortillas.

COVER tightly with foil and bake 20 minutes or until heated through.

Meanwhile, **PROCESS** avocados, sour cream, chiles, lemon juice, hot pepper sauce and salt in food processor or blender until smooth. Serve roll-ups with avocado sauce. *Makes 8 servings*

Cook's Nook: To reduce amount of fat in recipe, omit avocado sauce and serve with additional salsa and nonfat sour cream.

Ham Stromboli

1 can (10 ounces) refrigerated pizza dough
1 tablespoon prepared mustard
½ pound thinly sliced deli ham
1 package (3½ ounces) sliced pepperoni
1 teaspoon dried Italian seasoning
2 cups (8 ounces) shredded part-skim
    mozzarella cheese

1. Preheat oven to 425°F. Unroll pizza dough on greased jelly-roll pan; pat dough into 12-inch square.

2. Spread mustard over dough to within ½ inch of edges. Layer ham slices down center 6 inches of dough, leaving 3-inch border on either side and ½-inch border at top and bottom. Top ham with pepperoni slices. Sprinkle with Italian seasoning and cheese.

3. Fold sides of dough over filling, pinching center seam and top and bottom edges to seal. Bake 15 to 20 minutes or until lightly browned.

Makes 6 servings

Ham-Egg-Brie Strudel

4 eggs
1 tablespoon minced green onion
1 tablespoon minced parsley
¼ teaspoon salt
⅛ teaspoon black pepper
1 tablespoon vegetable oil
4 sheets phyllo pastry
2 tablespoons butter or margarine, melted
3 ounces sliced ham
3 ounces Brie cheese

1. Preheat oven to 375°F. Lightly beat eggs; add green onion, parsley, salt and pepper. Heat oil in medium skillet over medium-low heat. Add egg mixture; cook and stir until softly scrambled. Set aside.

2. Place 1 phyllo sheet on large piece of waxed paper. Brush lightly with butter. Top with second phyllo sheet; brush with butter. Repeat with remaining phyllo sheets. Arrange half of ham slices near short end of pastry, leaving 2-inch border around short end and sides. Place scrambled eggs over ham. Cut cheese into small pieces. Place over eggs; top with remaining ham.

3. Fold in long sides of phyllo; fold short end over ham. Use waxed paper to roll pastry to enclose filling. Place on lightly greased baking sheet, seam side down. Brush with remaining butter. Bake about 15 minutes or until lightly browned. Slice and serve immediately.

Makes 4 servings

Ham Stromboli

Tuscan Brunch Torta

3 cups all-purpose flour
¾ teaspoon salt
1 cup unsalted butter
6 to 8 tablespoons ice water
1 egg, separated
4 eggs
1 container (15 ounces) ricotta or light
    ricotta cheese
1 package (10 ounces) frozen chopped
    spinach, thawed and well drained
½ cup freshly grated Parmesan cheese
½ teaspoon red pepper flakes
⅛ teaspoon ground nutmeg
8 ounces sliced proscuitto or smoked ham
½ cup prepared pesto
1 jar (7 ounces) roasted red peppers, rinsed,
    drained and patted dry
4 ounces sliced Provolone cheese
1 tablespoon milk

1. Combine flour and salt in medium bowl. Cut in butter with pastry blender or 2 knives until mixture forms pea-sized pieces.

2. Add water, 1 tablespoon at a time, until dough forms a soft ball. Shape ⅔ of dough into disk; shape ⅓ of dough into another disk. Wrap each in plastic wrap; refrigerate 30 minutes or until firm enough to roll out.

3. Preheat oven to 375°F. Turn out large disk of dough onto lightly floured surface. Roll dough into 13-inch round. Transfer to 10-inch deep-dish pie plate; trim to ¼ inch beyond rim. Reserve scraps.

4. Pierce dough with fork about 40 times. Brush lightly with beaten egg white. Bake 10 minutes; cool on wire rack.

5. Beat 4 eggs lightly in large bowl. Add ricotta cheese, spinach, Parmesan cheese, red pepper flakes and nutmeg; mix well. Layer half of proscuitto over cooled crust; spread spinach mixture over proscuitto. Layer remaining proscuitto, pesto, roasted red peppers and Provolone cheese over top.

6. Roll out remaining dough to 12-inch round. Place over filling; trim to ½ inch beyond rim and flute edge. Reroll pastry scraps; cut into decorative shapes and place over pastry. Cut several slits on top of pastry to allow steam to escape.

7. Beat egg yolk and milk in small bowl with wire whisk; brush evenly over pastry. Place pie plate on baking sheet; bake 1 hour or until golden brown. Let cool on wire rack 15 minutes. Serve warm. *Makes 12 servings*

Tuscan Brunch Torta

Grilled Vegetable Muffuletta

10 cloves garlic, peeled
   Nonstick cooking spray
 1 tablespoon balsamic vinegar
 1 tablespoon fresh lemon juice
 1 tablespoon olive oil
 ¼ teaspoon ground black pepper
 1 round whole wheat sourdough bread loaf
      (1½ pounds)
 1 medium eggplant, cut crosswise into eight
      ¼-inch-thick slices
 2 small yellow squash, cut lengthwise into
      thin slices
 1 small red onion, thinly sliced
 1 large red bell pepper, seeded and quartered
 2 slices (1 ounce each) reduced-fat Swiss
      cheese
 8 washed spinach leaves

1. Preheat oven to 350°F. Place garlic in ovenproof dish. Spray garlic with cooking spray. Cover with foil; bake 30 to 35 minutes or until garlic is very soft and golden brown.

2. Place garlic, vinegar, lemon juice, olive oil and black pepper in food processor; process using on/off pulsing action until smooth. Set aside.

3. Slice top off bread loaf. Hollow out loaf, leaving ½-inch-thick shell. Reserve bread for another use.

4. Prepare coals for grilling. Brush vegetables with garlic mixture. Arrange on grid over medium coals. Grill 10 to 12 minutes or until crisp-tender, turning once. Separate onion slices into rings.

5. Layer half of eggplant, squash, onion, bell pepper, cheese and spinach in hollowed bread, pressing gently after each layer. Repeat layers with remaining vegetables, cheese and spinach. Replace bread top and serve immediately or wrap tightly with plastic wrap and refrigerate for up to 4 hours. Garnish as desired.   *Makes 6 servings*

Pita in the Morning

 1 teaspoon butter or margarine
 2 eggs, lightly beaten
 ¼ teaspoon salt
   Dash pepper
 1 whole wheat pita bread, cut in half
 ¼ cup alfalfa sprouts
 2 tablespoons shredded Cheddar cheese
 2 tablespoons chopped tomato
   Avocado slices (optional)

Microwave Directions:

1. Melt butter in microwavable 1-quart casserole at HIGH 30 seconds

2. Season eggs with salt and pepper. Add eggs to casserole. Microwave at HIGH 1½ to 2½ minutes, stirring once. Do not overcook; eggs should be soft with no liquid remaining.

3. Open pita to make pockets. Arrange sprouts in pockets. Divide eggs and cheese evenly between pockets. Top with tomato and avocado slices.
     Makes 1 sandwich

Grilled Vegetable Muffuletta

Monte Cristo Sandwiches

2 tablespoons honey mustard, divided
12 thin slices white or egg bread, divided
4 ounces sliced deli turkey breast
8 thin slices (4 ounces) Swiss cheese, divided
4 ounces smoked sliced deli ham, divided
2 eggs, beaten
¼ cup milk
1/16 teaspoon ground nutmeg
2 to 3 tablespoons butter or margarine
Powdered sugar
Strawberry or raspberry preserves

1. Preheat oven to 450°F.

2. To assemble 3-decker sandwich, spread ½ teaspoon mustard over 1 side of each of 3 bread slices. Place ¼ of turkey and 1 cheese slice over mustard on 1 bread slice. Top with second bread slice, mustard side up.

3. Place ¼ of ham and 1 cheese slice on top of bread. Top with remaining bread slice, mustard side down, pressing gently together. Repeat with remaining mustard, bread, turkey, cheese and ham to make 4 sandwiches.

4. Combine eggs, milk and nutmeg in shallow dish or pie plate.

5. Melt 1 tablespoon butter in large nonstick skillet over medium heat. Dip both sides of each sandwich briefly in egg mixture, letting excess drip back into dish.

6. Fry 1 sandwich at a time in skillet 4 minutes or until browned, turning halfway through cooking. Transfer sandwiches to greased or foil-lined baking sheet. Repeat with remaining sandwiches, adding butter to skillet as needed.

7. Bake sandwiches 5 to 7 minutes or until heated through and cheese is melted. Cut each sandwich in half diagonally; sprinkle lightly with powdered sugar. Serve immediately with preserves. *Makes 4 servings*

Monte Cristo Sandwich

Hearty
SANDWICH FARE

Thai Chicken Satays

1 cup plain yogurt
½ cup coconut milk
1 tablespoon curry powder
1 teaspoon lemon juice
1 teaspoon grated fresh ginger
½ teaspoon salt
½ teaspoon fresh ground black pepper
1 clove garlic, crushed
1 pound chicken tenders
6 (6-inch) pita bread rounds, cut in half
   Chopped fresh cilantro
   Plain yogurt

COMBINE 1 cup yogurt, coconut milk, curry, lemon juice, ginger, salt, pepper and garlic in medium bowl; reserve ⅓ cup marinade. Add chicken to remaining marinade; cover and refrigerate at least 8 hours.

SOAK 12 (10-inch) wooden skewers in water 30 minutes; set aside.

REMOVE chicken from marinade; discard marinade. Thread chicken onto skewers. Place skewers on broiler rack coated with nonstick cooking spray; place rack on broiler pan. Broil 4 to 5 inches from heat source 4 to 5 minutes. Turn skewers; brush with reserved marinade. Broil 4 minutes more or until chicken is no longer pink in center.

REMOVE chicken from skewers. Fill pitas with chicken and top with cilantro and dollop of yogurt. *Makes 6 servings*

Thai Chicken Satays

Chicken & Spinach Muffuletta

6 boneless skinless chicken breast halves
1 tablespoon olive oil
¼ cup prepared pesto
¼ cup chopped pitted black olives
¼ cup chopped green olives
1 round loaf (16 ounces) Hawaiian or
    French bread
2 cups fresh spinach leaves, washed
4 ounces sliced mozzarella cheese

SEASON chicken with salt and pepper. Heat oil in large skillet over medium heat until hot. Add chicken; cook 4 minutes on each side or until no longer pink in center. Cut cooked chicken into strips before assembling sandwich.

COMBINE pesto and olives in small bowl. Cut bread horizontally in half. Spread bottom half of bread with pesto mixture. Top with spinach, chicken, cheese and top of bread. Cut into wedges. *Makes 6 servings*

Walnut Chicken Salad Sandwiches

⅔ cup nonfat plain yogurt
½ cup finely chopped celery
½ cup finely chopped fresh spinach *or*
    3 tablespoons drained thawed frozen
    chopped spinach
¼ cup chopped green onions
1 tablespoon lemon juice
1 teaspoon ground mustard
1 tablespoon chopped fresh dill or tarragon
    or ½ teaspoon dried dill weed or
    tarragon leaves
3 cups diced cooked chicken breasts
1 apple, cored and diced
½ cup (2 ounces) chopped California
    walnuts
Salt and black pepper (optional)
4 pita breads, halved
4 iceberg lettuce leaves or other crisp
    lettuce leaves

In large bowl, combine yogurt, celery, spinach, onions, lemon juice, mustard and dill. Stir in chicken, apple and walnuts. Season with salt and pepper, if desired. Spoon ½ cup salad into each pita bread half; tuck in lettuce leaf.

Makes 4 sandwiches

Favorite recipe from **Walnut Marketing Board**

Chicken & Spinach Muffuletta

Stir-Fry Pita Sandwiches

12 ounces chicken tenders
1 onion, thinly sliced
1 red bell pepper, cut into strips
½ cup zesty Italian dressing
¼ teaspoon red pepper flakes
4 pita bread rounds
8 leaves leaf lettuce
4 tablespoons crumbled feta cheese

1. Cut chicken tenders in half lengthwise and crosswise. Coat large nonstick skillet with nonstick cooking spray. Cook and stir chicken over medium heat 3 minutes. Add onion and bell pepper; cook and stir 2 minutes. Add Italian dressing and red pepper flakes; cover and cook 3 minutes. Remove from heat; uncover and let cool 5 minutes.

2. While chicken cools, cut pita breads in half to form pockets. Line each pocket with lettuce leaf. Spoon chicken filling into pockets; sprinkle with feta cheese. *Makes 4 servings*

Prep and Cook Time: 17 minutes

Burrito Turkey Burgers

Vegetable cooking spray
2 pounds ground turkey
1 cup chopped onion
1 can (4 ounces) chopped green chilies, drained
1 package (1¼ ounces) taco seasoning mix
8 (8-inch) flour tortillas
1 can (16 ounces) nonfat refried beans
Shredded lettuce
½ cup shredded nonfat Cheddar cheese, divided
Salsa (optional)

1. Spray cold grill rack with vegetable cooking spray. Preheat charcoal grill for direct-heat cooking.

2. In medium bowl combine turkey, onion, chilies and seasoning mix. Shape turkey mixture into 8 (9×2-inch) rectangular-shaped burgers. Grill burgers 3 to 4 minutes; turn and continue cooking 2 to 3 minutes or until 160°F is reached on meat thermometer and meat is no longer pink in center. Remove and keep warm.

3. Heat tortillas according to package directions. Spread each tortilla with ¼ cup refried beans and sprinkle with lettuce. Place 1 burger in center of each tortilla and sprinkle with 1 tablespoon cheese. Fold sides of tortillas over burgers to create burritos. Serve with salsa, if desired.
Makes 8 servings

Favorite recipe from **National Turkey Federation**

Stir-Fry Pita Sandwich

Bistro Turkey Sandwiches

¼ cup reduced-calorie mayonnaise
2 tablespoons finely chopped fresh basil
2 tablespoons chopped drained sun-dried tomatoes in oil
2 tablespoons finely chopped pitted kalamata olives
⅛ teaspoon red pepper flakes
1 loaf focaccia bread, quartered and split *or* 8 slices sourdough bread
1 jar (7 ounces) roasted red bell peppers, rinsed and drained
4 romaine or red leaf lettuce leaves
2 packages (4 ounces each) HEBREW NATIONAL® Sliced Oven Roasted or Smoked Turkey Breast

Combine mayonnaise, basil, sun-dried tomatoes, olives and crushed red pepper in small bowl; mix well. Spread evenly over cut sides of bread. Remove excess liquid from roasted red bell peppers with paper towels. Layer roasted peppers, lettuce and turkey breast between bread slices.

Makes 4 servings

Grilled Chicken Pitas

1 container (8 ounces) plain lowfat yogurt
¾ cup WISH-BONE® Italian Dressing*
2 tablespoons chopped fresh parsley (optional)
1 pound boneless, skinless chicken breast halves or turkey cutlets
4 pita breads (6-inch rounds), halved
1 small cucumber, seeded and diced
1 medium tomato, diced
1½ cups shredded romaine or iceberg lettuce
4 ounces feta cheese, crumbled (optional)

*Also terrific with WISH-BONE® Robusto Italian or Lite Italian Dressing.

For marinade, blend yogurt, Italian dressing and parsley. Refrigerate ½ cup of the marinade for serving and ⅓ cup for brushing.

In large, shallow nonaluminum baking dish or plastic bag, pour remaining ¾ cup of the marinade over chicken; turn to coat. Cover dish, or close bag, and marinate in refrigerator, turning occasionally, up to 3 hours.

Remove chicken, discarding marinade. Grill or broil chicken, turning once and brushing occasionally with ⅓ cup refrigerated marinade, until chicken is no longer pink in center.

To serve, thinly slice chicken. Serve in bread halves with cucumber, tomato, lettuce and cheese. Drizzle with remaining ½ cup refrigerated marinade.

Makes 4 servings

Bistro Turkey Sandwich

Mediterranean Chicken Salad Sandwiches

4 boneless skinless chicken breast halves
1 teaspoon dried basil leaves
¼ teaspoon salt
¼ teaspoon black pepper
1 cup chopped cucumber
½ cup mayonnaise
¼ cup chopped roasted red pepper
¼ cup pitted black olive slices
¼ cup yogurt
¼ teaspoon garlic powder
6 Kaiser rolls, split
  Additional mayonnaise
  Lettuce leaves

PLACE chicken, ½ cup water, basil, salt and pepper in medium saucepan; bring to a boil. Reduce heat; simmer covered 10 to 12 minutes or until chicken is no longer pink in center. Remove chicken from saucepan; cool. Cut into ½-inch pieces.

COMBINE chicken, cucumber, mayonnaise, red pepper, olives, yogurt and garlic powder in medium bowl; toss to coat well.

SPREAD rolls with additional mayonnaise. Top with lettuce and chicken salad mixture.

Makes 6 servings

Turkey Picatta on Grilled Rolls

¼ cup lemon juice
¼ cup olive oil
2 tablespoons capers in liquid, chopped
2 cloves garlic, pressed
  Black pepper
1 pound turkey breast slices
4 soft French rolls, cut into halves
4 thin slices mozzarella or Swiss cheese
    (optional)
  Lettuce (optional)
  Red bell pepper slivers (optional)
  Additional capers (optional)

Combine lemon juice, oil, 2 tablespoons capers with liquid, garlic and black pepper to taste in shallow glass dish or large resealable plastic food storage bag. Add turkey; turn to coat. Cover and marinate in refrigerator several hours or overnight. Remove turkey from marinade; discard marinade. Lightly oil grid to prevent sticking. Grill turkey over medium-hot KINGSFORD® briquets 2 minutes or until turkey is no longer pink, turning once. Move cooked turkey slices to edge of grill to keep warm. Grill rolls, cut sides down, until toasted. Fill rolls with hot turkey slices, dividing equally. Add cheese, lettuce, bell pepper and additional capers, if desired.

Makes 4 servings

*Mediterranean Chicken
Salad Sandwich*

Easy Oriental Chicken Sandwiches

¼ cup peanut butter
2 tablespoons honey
2 tablespoons reduced-sodium soy sauce
½ teaspoon ground ginger
½ teaspoon garlic powder
¼ teaspoon ground red pepper
4 boneless skinless chicken breast halves
4 onion or Kaiser rolls, split
  Lettuce leaves
1 cup sliced cucumbers
1 cup bean sprouts
¼ cup sliced green onions

PREHEAT oven to 400°F. Combine peanut butter, honey, soy sauce, ginger, garlic powder and red pepper in small bowl; stir until well blended. Reserve ¼ cup peanut sauce.

PLACE chicken on foil-lined baking sheet. Spread remaining peanut sauce over chicken. Bake 20 minutes or until chicken is no longer pink in center.

FILL rolls with lettuce, cucumbers, bean sprouts and chicken; sprinkle with green onions. Serve with reserved peanut sauce.   *Makes 4 servings*

Turkey and Veggie Pita Pockets

12 ounces cooked turkey breast, coarsely chopped
1½ cups shredded zucchini
1 cup fresh mushrooms, thinly sliced
¾ cup mozzarella cheese, shredded
½ cup red bell pepper, cut into 1×¼-inch strips
2 green onions, sliced
½ teaspoon salt
½ teaspoon black pepper
3 pita pocket breads (6-inch size), cut in half

1. Combine turkey, zucchini, mushrooms, cheese, bell pepper, green onions, salt and black pepper in medium bowl. Cover and refrigerate at least 1 hour or overnight to allow flavors to blend.

2. To serve, place 1 cup turkey mixture into each pita pocket half. (Leftover turkey mixture will keep up to 4 days in refrigerator.)

Makes 6 servings

Note: Pockets may also be served warm. To microwave, wrap pita pocket in paper towel; place on microwave-safe plate. Microwave on HIGH (100% power) 1 to 1½ minutes or until filling is warm.

Favorite recipe from **National Turkey Federation**

Easy Oriental Chicken Sandwich

Smoky Barbecued Beef Sandwiches

2 large onions, cut into thin slices
1 well-trimmed first cut whole beef brisket (about 3 pounds)
½ teaspoon salt
¾ cup beer (not dark)
½ cup firmly packed light brown sugar
½ cup ketchup
1 tablespoon plus 1½ teaspoons Worcestershire sauce
1 tablespoon plus 1½ teaspoons soy sauce
2 cloves garlic, minced
2 whole canned chipotle peppers in adobo sauce, finely chopped*
1 teaspoon adobo sauce from can**
6 hoagie or kaiser rolls, split and toasted

*Canned chipotle peppers can be found in the Mexican section of most supermarkets or gourmet food stores.

**For spicier flavor, add 1 to 2 teaspoons additional sauce.

1. Preheat oven to 325°F. Separate onion slices into rings. Place in bottom of large roasting pan.

2. Place brisket, fat side up, over onions; sprinkle with salt. Combine remaining ingredients except rolls in 2- or 4-cup glass measuring cup; pour over brisket.

3. Cover with heavy-duty foil or roasting pan lid. Roast in oven 3 to 3½ hours until brisket is fork-tender.

4. Transfer brisket to cutting board, leaving sauce in pan; tent brisket with foil. Let stand 10 minutes. (Brisket and sauce may be prepared to this point; cool and cover separately. Refrigerate up to 1 day before serving.)

5. Skim fat from pan juices with large spoon; discard. Transfer juices to large saucepan. Cook over medium heat until thickened, stirring frequently.

6. Trim fat from brisket; carve across the grain into thin slices. Return slices to sauce; cook until heated through, coating slices with sauce. Serve slices and sauce in rolls.   *Makes 6 servings*

French Dip Sandwiches

½ cup A.1.® Original or A.1.® Bold & Spicy Steak Sauce, divided
1 tablespoon GREY POUPON® Dijon Mustard
4 steak rolls, split horizontally
8 ounces sliced cooked roast beef
1 (13¾-fluid-ounce) can beef broth

In small bowl, blend ¼ cup steak sauce and mustard; spread mixture evenly on cut sides of roll tops. Arrange 2 ounces beef on each roll bottom; replace roll tops over beef. Slice sandwiches in half crosswise if desired. In small saucepan, heat broth and remaining ¼ cup steak sauce, stirring occasionally. Serve as a dipping sauce with sandwiches. Garnish as desired.

Makes 4 servings

Smoky Barbecued Beef Sandwich

Blue Cheese Burgers with Red Onion

2 pounds ground chuck
2 cloves garlic, minced
1 teaspoon salt
½ teaspoon black pepper
4 ounces blue cheese
⅓ cup coarsely chopped walnuts, toasted
1 torpedo (long) red onion *or* 2 small red
    onions, sliced into ⅜-inch-thick rounds
2 baguettes (each 12 inches long)
    Olive or vegetable oil

Combine beef, garlic, salt and pepper in medium bowl. Shape meat mixture into 12 oval patties. Mash cheese and blend with walnuts in small bowl. Divide cheese mixture equally; place onto centers of 6 meat patties. Top with remaining meat patties; tightly pinch edges together to seal in filling.

Oil hot grid to help prevent sticking. Grill patties and onion, if desired, on covered grill, over medium KINGSFORD® briquets, 7 to 12 minutes for medium doneness, turning once. Cut baguettes into 4-inch lengths; split each piece and brush cut side with olive oil. Move cooked burgers to edge of grill to keep warm. Grill bread, oil side down, until lightly toasted. Serve burgers on toasted baguettes. *Makes 6 servings*

Rice and Roast Beef Sandwiches

1 small red onion, sliced into thin rings
1 teaspoon olive oil
3 cups cooked brown rice
½ cup whole kernel corn
½ cup sliced ripe olives (optional)
½ cup barbecue sauce
2 tablespoons lime juice
½ teaspoon ground cumin
½ teaspoon garlic salt
4 whole-wheat pita rounds, halved and
    warmed
8 lettuce leaves
1 cup sliced, cooked lean roast beef
1 large tomato, seeded and chopped

Cook onion in oil in large skillet over medium-high heat until tender. Add rice, corn, olives, barbecue sauce, lime juice, cumin and garlic salt; toss until heated. Line each pita half with lettuce leaf, ½ cup hot rice mixture and roast beef; top with tomato. *Makes 8 (½-pita) sandwiches*

Favorite recipe from **USA Rice Federation**

Blue Cheese Burger with Red Onion

Barbecued Pork Tenderloin Sandwiches

½ **cup ketchup**
⅓ **cup packed brown sugar**
2 **tablespoons bourbon or whiskey
(optional)**
1 **tablespoon Worcestershire sauce**
½ **teaspoon dry mustard**
¼ **teaspoon ground red pepper**
1 **clove garlic, minced**
2 **whole pork tenderloins (about ¾ pound
each), well trimmed**
1 **large red onion, cut into 6 (¼-inch-thick)
slices**
6 **hoagie rolls or Kaiser rolls, split**

1. Prepare barbecue grill for direct cooking.

2. Combine ketchup, sugar, bourbon, Worcestershire sauce, mustard, ground red pepper and garlic in small, heavy saucepan with ovenproof handle; mix well.

3. Set saucepan on one side of grid.* Place tenderloins on center of grid. Grill tenderloins, on uncovered grill, over medium-hot coals 8 minutes. Simmer sauce 5 minutes or until thickened, stirring occasionally.

4. Turn tenderloins with tongs; continue to grill, uncovered, 5 minutes. Add onion slices to grid. Set aside half of sauce; reserve. Brush tenderloins and onion with a portion of remaining sauce.

5. Continue to grill, uncovered, 7 to 10 minutes or until tenderloins are juicy and barely pink in center, brushing with remaining sauce and turning onion and tenderloins halfway through grilling time. (If desired, insert instant-read thermometer** into center of thickest part of tenderloins. Thermometer should register 160°F.)

6. Carve tenderloins crosswise into thin slices; separate onion slices into rings. Divide meat and onion rings among rolls; drizzle with reserved sauce.   *Makes 6 servings*

*If desired, sauce may be prepared on range-top. Combine ketchup, sugar, bourbon, Worcestershire sauce, mustard, ground red pepper and garlic in small saucepan. Bring to a boil over medium-high heat. Reduce heat to low and simmer, uncovered, 5 minutes or until thickened, stirring occasionally.

**Do not leave instant-read thermometer in tenderloins during grilling since the thermometer is not heatproof.

*Barbecued Pork
Tenderloin Sandwich*

Grilled Feta Burgers

½ pound lean ground sirloin
½ pound ground turkey breast
2 teaspoons grated lemon peel
1 teaspoon olive oil
1 teaspoon dried oregano leaves
¼ teaspoon salt
⅛ teaspoon ground black pepper
1 ounce feta cheese
   Cucumber Raita (recipe follows)
4 slices tomato
4 whole wheat hamburger buns

1. Combine sirloin, turkey, lemon peel, oil, oregano, salt and pepper; mix well and shape into 8 patties. Make small depression in each of 4 patties and place ¼ of the cheese in each depression. Cover each with remaining 4 patties, sealing edges to form burgers.

2. Grill burgers 10 to 12 minutes or until thoroughly cooked, turning once. Serve with Cucumber Raita and tomato slice on whole wheat bun.   *Makes 4 burgers*

Cucumber Raita

1 cup plain nonfat yogurt
½ cup finely chopped cucumber
1 tablespoon minced fresh mint leaves
1 clove garlic, minced
¼ teaspoon salt

1. Combine all ingredients in small bowl. Cover and refrigerate until ready to use.

Cuban-Style Steak Sandwiches

1½ pounds sandwich steaks (thinly sliced top loin)
3 tablespoons olive oil, divided
1 tablespoon lime juice
1½ teaspoons minced garlic
½ teaspoon dried thyme leaves
¼ teaspoon salt
¼ teaspoon black pepper
1 large onion, cut in half and thinly sliced
4 hoagie or submarine sandwich rolls (8 inches), split
   Lettuce leaves
1 tomato, sliced

1. Cut steaks into 3- to 4-inch pieces. Combine steaks with 2 tablespoons oil, lime juice, garlic, thyme, salt and pepper in shallow dish; toss to coat.

2. Heat skillet over high heat 1 minute. Cook steaks in 2 batches, 1½ minutes per side. Remove from pan and cover to keep warm.

3. Add remaining 1 tablespoon oil and onion to skillet. Cook 3 minutes or until tender and lightly browned. Fill rolls with lettuce, tomato, steak and onion.   *Makes 4 servings*

Prep and Cook Time: 18 minutes

Grilled Feta Burger

Nutty Albacore Salad Pitas

1 can (6 ounces) STARKIST® Solid White
    Tuna, drained and flaked
½ cup mayonnaise
⅓ cup chopped celery
¼ cup raisins or seedless grape halves
¼ cup chopped walnuts, pecans or almonds
½ teaspoon dried dill weed
    Salt and pepper to taste
2 pita breads, halved
4 curly leaf lettuce leaves

In medium bowl, combine tuna, mayonnaise, celery, raisins, nuts and dill; mix well. Add salt and pepper. Line each pita bread half with lettuce leaf; fill each with ¼ of tuna mixture.

Makes 4 servings

Prep Time: 10 minutes

Cajun Catfish Sandwiches

    Aioli Tartar Sauce (recipe follows)
4½ teaspoons paprika
1 tablespoon dried oregano leaves
1½ teaspoons salt
¾ teaspoon granulated garlic
½ teaspoon white pepper
½ teaspoon black pepper
½ teaspoon cayenne pepper
4 small catfish fillets (1¼ pounds)
    Lemon juice
4 sourdough rolls, split
4 cups finely shredded cabbage
    Lemon wedges

Prepare Aioli Tartar Sauce; set aside. Combine paprika, oregano, salt, garlic and peppers until blended. Brush catfish with lemon juice; sprinkle evenly with seasoning mix to coat. Lightly oil grid to prevent sticking. Grill over medium-hot KINGSFORD® briquets, allowing 10 minutes cooking time for each inch of thickness, turning once. Spread Aioli Tartar Sauce onto insides of rolls. Top each roll with catfish fillet and 1 cup cabbage. Serve with lemon wedges.

Makes 4 sandwiches

Aioli Tartar Sauce: Prepare Grilled Garlic (page 170). Combine ½ cup mayonnaise, 12 mashed cloves Grilled Garlic, 2 teaspoons each lemon juice and chopped parsley, and 1 teaspoon chopped, drained capers; blend well.

Nutty Albacore Salad Pita

Shrimp Pitas

¾ cup olive oil
½ cup red wine vinegar
2 medium onions, chopped and divided
2 cloves garlic, minced and divided
2 teaspoons Italian seasoning, divided
1 pound medium shrimp, peeled and deveined
2 medium red or green bell peppers, julienned
4 cups fresh spinach leaves, stems removed and torn
3 cups cooked brown rice
1 teaspoon salt
½ teaspoon ground black pepper
3 pieces pita bread (about 6 inches), each cut in half

Combine olive oil, vinegar, ½ cup chopped onion, 1 clove garlic and 1 teaspoon Italian seasoning in large bowl. Add shrimp; stir until well coated. Cover and marinate in refrigerator 4 hours or overnight.

Thoroughly drain shrimp; discard marinade. Heat large skillet over medium-high heat until hot. Add shrimp, remaining onion, bell peppers, spinach and remaining 1 clove garlic; sauté 3 to 5 minutes or until shrimp are no longer pink and spinach is wilted. Add rice, remaining 1 teaspoon Italian seasoning, salt and black pepper. Cook and stir 2 to 3 minutes or until flavors are well blended. To serve, fill each pita with ½ to ¾ cup rice mixture.   *Makes 6 servings*

Favorite recipe from **USA Rice Federation**

Tuna Monte Cristo Sandwiches

4 thin slices (2 ounces) Cheddar cheese
4 slices sour dough or challah (egg) bread
½ pound deli tuna salad
1 egg, beaten
¼ cup milk
2 tablespoons butter or margarine

1. Place 1 slice cheese on each bread slice. Spread tuna salad evenly over two slices of cheese-topped bread. Close sandwiches with remaining bread slices.

2. Combine egg and milk in shallow bowl. Dip sandwiches in egg mixture, turning to coat well.

3. Melt butter in large nonstick skillet over medium heat. Add sandwiches; cook 4 to 5 minutes per side or until bread is golden brown and cheese is melted.   *Makes 2 servings*

Serve sandwiches with tortilla chips and a chilled fresh fruit salad.

Prep and Cook Time: 20 minutes

Grilled Vegetable Sandwiches with Garlic Mayonnaise

⅓ cup mayonnaise
2 cloves garlic, minced
2 large red bell peppers, cored and quartered
1 small eggplant, cut into ¼-inch slices
   Vegetable oil
8 slices country-style bread

1. Prepare barbecue grill for direct cooking.

2. Blend mayonnaise and garlic in small bowl; set aside.

3. Spray barbecue grid with nonstick cooking spray. Place bell peppers and eggplant on prepared grid. Brush vegetables with oil and season with salt and black pepper to taste.

4. Grill vegetables, on covered grill, over medium-hot coals 10 minutes or until fork-tender, turning halfway through grilling time.

5. Spread desired amount of mayonnaise mixture on each bread slice. Top 4 bread slices with equal amounts of grilled vegetables; cover with remaining bread. Cut each sandwich in half. Serve immediately. *Makes 4 servings*

Prep and cook time: 25 minutes

Italian Vegetable Pockets

1 medium eggplant (about ¾ pound)
1 small zucchini
1 small yellow squash
4 ripe plum tomatoes
1⅓ cups (2.8 ounce can) FRENCH'S® French Fried Onions
2 tablespoons olive oil
2 tablespoons FRENCH'S® Worcestershire Sauce
2 teaspoons Italian seasoning
2 teaspoons seasoned salt
1 teaspoon garlic powder

Cut eggplant, zucchini, squash and tomatoes into bite-size chunks; place in large bowl. Add French Fried Onions. Whisk together oil, Worcestershire and seasonings in small bowl. Pour over vegetables. Toss well to coat evenly. Cut six 12-inch circles of heavy-duty foil. Spoon about 2 cups vegetables in center of each piece of foil. Fold foil in half over vegetables. Seal edges securely with tight double folds.

Place packets on grid. Cook over hot coals 15 minutes or until vegetables are tender, opening foil packets carefully. Serve warm.
Makes 6 side-dish servings

Prep Time: 15 minutes
Cook Time: 15 minutes

Grilled Vegetable Sandwich with Garlic Mayonnaise

Grilled Vegetable & Cheese Sandwiches

2 large zucchini squash, cut lengthwise into
    eight ¼-inch slices
4 slices sweet onion (such as Vidalia or
    Walla Walla) cut ¼ inch thick
1 large yellow bell pepper, cut lengthwise
    into quarters
6 tablespoons light or regular Caesar salad
    dressing, divided
8 oval slices sourdough bread
6 (1-ounce) slices Muenster cheese

1. Prepare barbecue for grilling. Brush both sides of vegetables with ¼ cup dressing. Place vegetables on grid over medium coals. Grill on covered grill 5 minutes. Turn; grill 2 minutes.

2. Brush both sides of bread lightly with remaining 2 tablespoons dressing. Place bread around vegetables; grill 2 minutes or until bread is lightly toasted. Turn bread; top 4 pieces of bread with 4 slices of cheese. Tear remaining 2 cheese slices into small pieces; place on bread around cheese. Grill vegetables and bread 1 to 2 minutes more or until cheese is melted, bread is toasted and vegetables are crisp-tender.

3. Arrange vegetables over cheese side of bread; top with remaining bread. *Makes 4 servings*

Serving Suggestion: Serve with a fresh fruit salad.

Prep and Cook Time: 22 minutes

Eggplant & Pepper Cheese Sandwiches

1 (8-ounce) eggplant, cut into 18 slices
    Salt and black pepper, to taste
⅓ cup GREY POUPON® COUNTRY
    DIJON® Mustard
¼ cup olive oil
2 tablespoons REGINA® Red Wine Vinegar
¾ teaspoon dried oregano leaves
1 clove garlic, crushed
6 (4-inch) pieces French bread, cut in half
1 (7-ounce) jar roasted red peppers, cut into
    strips
1½ cups shredded mozzarella cheese
    (6 ounces)

Place eggplant slices on greased baking sheet, overlapping slightly. Sprinkle lightly with salt and pepper. Bake at 400°F for 10 to 12 minutes or until tender.

Blend mustard, oil, vinegar, oregano and garlic. Brush eggplant slices with ¼ cup mustard mixture; broil eggplant for 1 minute.

Brush cut sides of French bread with remaining mustard mixture. Layer 3 slices eggplant, a few red pepper strips and ¼ cup cheese on each bread bottom. Place on broiler pan with roll tops, cut-sides up; broil until cheese melts. Close sandwiches with bread tops and serve immediately; garnish as desired.

Makes 6 sandwiches

*Grilled Vegetable & Cheese
Sandwiches*

Caramelized Onion & Eggplant Sandwiches

Grilled Garlic Aioli (recipe follows) or
   mayonnaise
½ cup packed brown sugar
½ cup water
½ cup soy sauce
2 tablespoons molasses
5 slices fresh ginger
¼ teaspoon ground coriander
   Dash black pepper
1 large yellow onion
4 large eggplant slices, 1 inch thick
4 round buns, split
4 tomato slices
   Mixed greens
   Radishes
   Carrot curls

Prepare Grilled Garlic Aioli; set aside. Combine sugar, water, soy sauce, molasses, ginger, coriander and pepper in small saucepan. Bring to boil, stirring constantly. Reduce heat; simmer marinade 5 minutes, stirring occasionally. Cool. Cut onion into ½-inch-thick slices. Insert wooden picks into onion slices from edges to prevent separating into rings. (Soak wooden picks in hot water 15 minutes to prevent burning.) Marinate eggplant and onion in marinade 10 to 15 minutes. Remove vegetables from marinade; reserve marinade. Lightly oil grid to prevent sticking. Grill vegetables on covered grill around edge of medium-hot KINGSFORD® briquets about 20 minutes or until tender, turning once or twice and brushing with reserved marinade. Place buns on grill, cut sides down, until toasted. Serve eggplant and onion on grilled buns with tomato, greens and Grilled Garlic Aioli. Garnish with radishes and carrot curls. *Makes 4 sandwiches*

Grilled Garlic Aioli: Prepare Grilled Garlic (recipe follows). Mash 8 cloves Grilled Garlic in small bowl. Add ¼ cup mayonnaise; mix until blended.

Grilled Garlic: Peel outermost papery skin from 1 or 2 garlic heads. Brush heads with olive oil. Grill heads at edge of grid on covered grill over medium-hot KINGSFORD® briquets 30 to 40 minutes or until cloves are soft and buttery. Cool slightly. Gently squeeze softened garlic head from root end so that cloves slip out of stems into small bowl. Use immediately or cover and refrigerate up to 1 week.

Caramelized Onion &
Eggplant Sandwich

Healthy
WRAPS & MORE

Crowd-Pleasing Burritos

1 pound (2½ cups) dried pinto beans, rinsed
6 cups water
2 cups chopped onions
4 cloves garlic, minced
3 jalapeño peppers,* seeded and minced
2 teaspoons salt
16 (10-inch) flour tortillas
4 cups shredded iceberg lettuce
4 cups shredded romaine lettuce leaves
2 cups (8 ounces) reduced-fat Cheddar
    cheese
2 cups salsa
1 cup reduced-fat sour cream
1 cup minced cilantro

*Jalapeño peppers can sting and irritate the skin; wear rubber gloves when handling peppers and do not touch eyes. Wash hands after handling.

1. Place beans in Dutch oven. Cover with 2 inches of water. Bring to a boil; reduce heat to low. Simmer 5 minutes. Remove from heat and let stand, covered, 1 hour. Drain liquid from beans.

2. Add 6 cups water, onions, garlic, peppers and salt. Bring to a boil; reduce heat to low. Simmer, covered, 1 hour or until beans are tender. Drain cooking broth from beans.

3. Preheat oven to 300°F. Stack tortillas and wrap in foil. Bake 20 minutes or until heated through.

4. Combine lettuces. Top tortillas with bean mixture, lettuces, cheese, salsa, sour cream and cilantro. Fold in 2 sides; roll to enclose filling. Garnish as desired.   *Makes 16 servings*

Nutrients per Serving:

Calories: 276, Total Fat: 6 g, Cholesterol: 12 mg, Sodium: 699 mg

Crowd-Pleasing Burrito

Fajitas

Fajita Marinade (recipe follows)
1 pound flank steak
4 bell peppers, any color, halved
1 large bunch green onions
12 (7-inch) flour tortillas
Salsa Cruda (recipe follows)
1 cup coarsely chopped fresh cilantro
1 ripe avocado, thinly sliced (optional)
6 tablespoons low-fat sour cream (optional)

1. Prepare Fajita Marinade. Combine Fajita Marinade and flank steak in large resealable plastic food storage bag. Press air from bag and seal. Refrigerate 30 minutes or up to 24 hours.

2. Wrap tortillas in foil in stacks of 3; set aside.

3. Drain marinade from meat into small saucepan. Bring to a boil over high heat. Remove from heat.

4. Spray cold grid of grill with nonstick cooking spray. Adjust grid 4 to 6 inches above heat. Preheat grill to medium-high heat. Place meat in center of grid. Place peppers, skin side down, around meat; cover. Grill peppers 6 minutes or until skin is spotted with brown. Turn over and continue grilling 6 to 8 minutes or until tender. Move to sides of grill to keep warm while meat finishes grilling. Grill meat, basting frequently with marinade, 8 minutes or until browned on bottom. Turn over; grill 8 to 10 minutes or until slightly pink in center. During the last 4 minutes of grilling, brush green onions with remaining marinade and place on grid; grill 1 to 2 minutes or until browned in spots. Turn over; grill 1 to 2 minutes or until tender.

5. Place tortillas on grid; heat about 5 minutes. Slice peppers and onions into thin 2-inch-long pieces. Thinly slice meat across the grain.

6. Place each tortilla on plate. Place meat, peppers, onions, Salsa Cruda and cilantro in center of each tortilla. Fold bottom 3 inches of each tortilla up over filling; fold sides completely over filling to enclose. Serve with avocado and sour cream, if desired. *Makes 6 servings*

Fajita Marinade

½ cup lime juice *or* ¼ cup lime juice and
¼ cup tequilla or beer
1 tablespoon dried oregano leaves
1 tablespoon minced garlic
2 teaspoons ground cumin
2 teaspoons black pepper

1. Combine lime juice, oregano, garlic, cumin and black pepper in 1-cup glass measure.

Salsa Cruda

1 cup chopped tomato
2 tablespoons minced onion
2 tablespoons minced fresh cilantro (optional)
2 tablespoons lime juice
½ jalapeño pepper, seeded and minced
1 clove garlic, minced

1. Combine tomato, onion, cilantro, lime juice, jalapeño pepper and garlic in small bowl.

Nutrients per Serving:

Calories: 304, Total Fat: 9 g, Cholesterol: 44 mg, Sodium: 198 mg

Chicken Fajitas

      1 pound chicken tenders
   ¼ cup lime juice
      4 cloves garlic, minced, divided
      1 cup sliced red bell peppers
      1 cup sliced green bell peppers
      1 cup sliced yellow bell peppers
   ¾ cup onion slices (about 1 medium)
   ½ teaspoon ground cumin
   ¼ teaspoon salt
   ¼ teaspoon ground red pepper
      8 teaspoons low-fat sour cream
      8 (6-inch) flour tortillas, warmed
         Green onion tops (optional)
         Salsa (optional)

1. Arrange chicken in 11×7-inch glass baking dish; add lime juice and 2 cloves minced garlic. Toss to coat. Cover; marinate in refrigerator 30 minutes, stirring occasionally.

2. Spray large nonstick skillet with nonstick cooking spray; heat over medium heat until hot. Add chicken mixture; cook and stir 5 to 7 minutes or until browned and no longer pink in center. Remove chicken from skillet. Drain excess liquid from skillet, if necessary.

3. Add bell peppers, onion and remaining 2 cloves minced garlic to skillet; cook and stir about 5 minutes or until tender. Sprinkle with cumin, salt and ground red pepper. Return chicken to skillet. Cook and stir 1 to 2 minutes.

4. Spread 1 teaspoon sour cream on each tortilla. Top with chicken mixture; roll up. Tie with green onion tops and serve with salsa, if desired.

Makes 4 servings

Nutrients per Serving:

Calories: 382, Total Fat: 7 g, Cholesterol: 60 mg, Sodium: 421 mg

Beef & Bean Burritos

   ½ pound beef round steak, cut into ½-inch
         pieces
      3 cloves garlic, minced
      1 can (about 15 ounces) pinto beans, rinsed
         and drained
      1 can (4 ounces) diced mild green chilies,
         drained
   ¼ cup finely chopped cilantro
      6 (6-inch) flour tortillas
   ½ cup (2 ounces) shredded reduced-fat
         Cheddar cheese

1. Spray nonstick skillet with nonstick cooking spray; heat over medium heat until hot. Add steak and garlic; cook and stir 5 minutes or until steak is cooked to desired doneness. Stir beans, chilies and cilantro into skillet; cook and stir 5 minutes or until heated through.

2. Spoon steak mixture evenly down center of each tortilla; sprinkle with cheese. Fold bottom end of tortilla over filling; roll to enclose. Garnish, if desired.

Makes 6 servings

Nutrients per Serving:

Calories: 278, Total Fat: 7 g, Cholesterol: 31 mg, Sodium: 956 mg

Chicken Fajitas

Turkey Gyros

1 turkey tenderloin (8 ounces)
1½ teaspoons Greek seasoning
1 cucumber
⅔ cup plain nonfat yogurt
¼ cup finely chopped onion
2 teaspoons dried dill weed
2 teaspoons fresh lemon juice
1 teaspoon olive oil
4 pita breads
1½ cups washed and shredded romaine lettuce
1 tomato, thinly sliced
2 tablespoons crumbled feta cheese

1. Cut turkey tenderloin across the grain into ¼-inch slices. Place turkey slices on plate; lightly sprinkle both sides with Greek seasoning. Let stand 5 minutes.

2. Cut two thirds of cucumber into thin slices. Finely chop remaining cucumber. Combine chopped cucumber, yogurt, onion, dill weed and lemon juice in small bowl.

3. Heat olive oil in large skillet over medium heat until hot. Add turkey. Cook 2 minutes on each side or until cooked through. Wrap 2 pita breads in paper towel. Microwave at HIGH 30 seconds or just until warmed. Repeat with remaining pita breads.

4. Divide lettuce, tomato, cucumber slices, turkey, cheese and yogurt-cucumber sauce evenly among pita breads. Fold edges over and secure with wooden picks.   *Makes 4 servings*

Nutrients per Serving:

Calories: 319, Total Fat: 4 g, Cholesterol: 55 mg, Sodium: 477 mg

Hummus Pita Sandwiches

2 tablespoons sesame seeds
1 can (15 ounces) chick-peas
1 to 2 cloves garlic, peeled
¼ cup loosely packed parsley sprigs
3 tablespoons fresh lemon juice
1 tablespoon olive oil
¼ teaspoon coarsely ground black pepper
4 pita breads
2 tomatoes, thinly sliced
1 cucumber, sliced
1 cup alfalfa sprouts, rinsed and drained
2 tablespoons crumbled feta cheese

1. Toast sesame seeds in small nonstick skillet over medium heat until lightly browned, stirring frequently. Remove from skillet and cool. Drain chick-peas; reserve liquid.

2. Place garlic in food processor. Process until minced. Add chick-peas, parsley, lemon juice, olive oil and pepper. Process until almost smooth, scraping sides of bowl once. If mixture is very thick, add 1 to 2 tablespoons reserved chick-pea liquid. Pour hummus into medium bowl. Stir in sesame seeds.

3. Cut pita breads in half. Spread about 3 tablespoons hummus in each pita bread half. Divide tomatoes, cucumber slices and alfalfa sprouts evenly among pita breads. Sprinkle with feta cheese.   *Makes 4 servings*

Nutrients per Serving:

Calories: 364, Total Fat:9 g, Cholesterol: 7 mg, Sodium: 483 mg

Turkey Gyro

Grilled Flank Steak with Horseradish Sauce

1 pound beef flank steak
2 tablespoons low sodium soy sauce
1 tablespoon red wine vinegar
2 cloves garlic, minced
½ teaspoon pepper
1 cup nonfat sour cream
1 tablespoon prepared horseradish
1 tablespoon Dijon mustard
¼ cup finely chopped fresh parsley
½ teaspoon salt
6 sourdough rolls, split
6 romaine lettuce leaves

1. Place flank steak in large resealable plastic food storage bag. Add soy sauce, vinegar, garlic and pepper. Close bag securely; turn to coat. Marinate in refrigerator at least 1 hour.

2. Prepare grill or preheat broiler. Drain steak; discard marinade. Grill or broil over medium-high heat 5 minutes. Turn beef; grill 6 minutes for medium-rare or until desired doneness. Cover with foil; let stand 15 minutes. Thinly slice steak across grain.

3. Combine sour cream, horseradish, mustard, parsley and salt in small bowl until well blended. Spread rolls with horseradish sauce; layer with sliced steak and lettuce. Garnish with small pickles, if desired. *Makes 6 servings*

Nutrients per Serving:

Calories: 220, Total Fat: 6 g, Cholesterol: 35 mg, Sodium: 542 mg

Broiled Turkey Burgers

1 pound ground turkey
¼ cup finely chopped green onions
¼ cup finely chopped parsley
2 tablespoons dry red wine
1 teaspoon Italian seasoning
¼ teaspoon salt
¼ teaspoon black pepper
4 whole wheat hamburger buns

1. Preheat broiler.

2. Combine turkey, green onions, parsley, wine, Italian seasoning, salt and pepper in large bowl; mix well. Shape turkey mixture into 4 (¾-inch-thick) burgers.

3. Spray rack of broiler pan with nonstick cooking spray; place burgers on rack. Broil burgers, 4 inches from heat source, 5 to 6 minutes per side or until burgers are no longer pink in centers. Serve on whole wheat buns.
Makes 4 servings

Serving Suggestion: Serve burgers with lettuce, grilled pineapple slice and bell pepper strips, if desired.

Nutrients per Serving:

Calories: 243, Total Fat: 3g, Cholesterol: 74 mg, Sodium: 384 mg

Chicken and Mozzarella Melts

2 cloves garlic, crushed
4 boneless skinless chicken breast halves
(¾ pound)
⅛ teaspoon salt
⅛ teaspoon pepper
1 tablespoon prepared pesto sauce
4 small hard rolls, split
12 fresh spinach leaves
8 fresh basil leaves* (optional)
3 plum tomatoes, sliced
½ cup (2 ounces) shredded part-skim
mozzarella cheese

*Omit basil leaves if fresh are unavailable. Do not substitute dried basil leaves.

1. Preheat oven to 350°F. Rub garlic on chicken. Spray nonstick skillet with nonstick cooking spray; heat over medium heat. Cook chicken 5 to 6 minutes on each side or until no longer pink in center. Sprinkle with salt and pepper.

2. Brush pesto sauce on bottom halves of rolls; layer with spinach, basil, if desired, and tomatoes. Place chicken in rolls; sprinkle with cheese. (If desired, sandwiches may be prepared up to this point and wrapped in foil and refrigerated. Bake in preheated 350°F oven until chicken is warm, about 20 minutes.)

3. Wrap sandwiches in foil; bake 10 minutes or until cheese is melted.   *Makes 4 servings*

Nutrients per Serving:

Calories: 299, Total Fat: 5 g, Cholesterol: 47 mg, Sodium: 498 mg

Deviled Burgers

2 slices bread, finely chopped
¼ cup finely chopped onion
¼ cup tomato ketchup
1 tablespoon Worcestershire sauce
2 teaspoons prepared mustard
2 teaspoons creamy horseradish
½ teaspoon garlic powder
½ teaspoon chili powder
1 pound extra-lean ground beef
6 hamburger buns

1. Preheat broiler. Combine bread, onion, ketchup, Worcestershire sauce, mustard, horseradish, garlic powder and chili powder in large bowl until well blended. Gently blend ground beef into mixture. (Do not overwork.)

2. Shape mixture into 6 (3-inch) burgers. Place burgers on ungreased jelly-roll pan.

3. Broil burgers 4 inches from heat source 4 minutes per side or until desired doneness. Serve on hamburger buns. Garnish, if desired.
         Makes 6 servings

Nutrients per Serving:

Calories: 298, Total Fat: 9 g, Cholesterol: 50 mg, Sodium: 519 mg

Grilled Chicken Breast and Peperonata Sandwiches

1 tablespoon olive oil or vegetable oil
1 medium red bell pepper, sliced into strips
1 medium green bell pepper, sliced into strips
¾ cup onion slices (about 1 medium)
2 cloves garlic, minced
¼ teaspoon salt
¼ teaspoon black pepper
4 boneless skinless chicken breast halves (about 1 pound)
4 small French rolls, split and toasted

1. Heat oil in large nonstick skillet over medium heat until hot. Add bell peppers, onion and garlic; cook and stir 5 minutes. Reduce heat to low; cook and stir about 20 minutes or until vegetables are very soft. Sprinkle with salt and black pepper.

2. Grill chicken, on covered grill over medium-hot coals, 10 minutes on each side or until chicken is no longer pink in center. Or, broil chicken, 6 inches from heat source, 7 to 8 minutes on each side or until chicken is no longer pink in center.

3. Place chicken in rolls. Divide pepper mixture evenly; spoon over chicken.   *Makes 4 servings*

Nutrients per Serving:

Calories: 321, Total Fat: 8 g, Cholesterol: 58 mg, Sodium: 497 mg

Southwestern Sloppy Joes

1 pound lean ground round
1 cup chopped onion
¼ cup chopped celery
¼ cup water
1 can (10 ounces) diced tomatoes with green chilies
1 can (8 ounces) no-salt-added tomato sauce
4 teaspoons brown sugar
½ teaspoon ground cumin
¼ teaspoon salt
9 whole wheat hamburger buns

1. Heat large nonstick skillet over high heat. Add beef, onion, celery and water. Reduce heat to medium. Cook and stir 5 minutes or until meat is no longer pink. Drain fat.

2. Stir in tomatoes and green chilies, tomato sauce, brown sugar, cumin and salt; bring to a boil over high heat. Reduce heat; simmer 20 minutes or until mixture thickens. Serve on whole wheat buns. Garnish as desired.
      Makes 9 servings

Nutrients per Serving:

Calories: 190, Total Fat: 4 g, Cholesterol: 15 mg, Sodium: 413 mg

Grilled Chicken Breast and Peperonata Sandwich

Fresh Rockfish Burgers

8 ounces skinless rockfish or scrod fillet
1 egg white *or* 2 tablespoons egg substitute
¼ cup dry bread crumbs
1 green onion, finely chopped
1 tablespoon finely chopped parsley
2 teaspoons fresh lime juice
1½ teaspoons capers
1 teaspoon Dijon mustard
¼ teaspoon salt
⅛ teaspoon black pepper
Nonstick cooking spray
4 grilled whole wheat English muffins
4 leaf lettuce leaves
4 slices red or yellow tomato
Additional Dijon mustard for serving, if desired

1. Finely chop rockfish and place in medium bowl. Add egg white, bread crumbs, onion, parsley, lime juice, capers, mustard, salt and pepper; gently combine with fork. Shape into 4 patties.

2. Spray heavy grillproof cast iron skillet or griddle with nonstick cooking spray; place on grid over hot coals to heat. Spray tops of burgers with additional cooking spray. Place burgers in hot skillet; grill on covered grill over hot coals 4 to 5 minutes or until burgers are browned on both sides, turning once. Serve on English muffins or buns with lettuce, tomato slice and Dijon mustard, if desired.   *Makes 4 servings*

Nutrients per Serving:

Calories: 227, Total Fat: 3 g, Cholesterol: 19 mg, Sodium: 720 mg

Barbecued Pork Sandwiches

2 pork tenderloins (about 1½ pounds total)
⅓ cup prepared barbecue sauce
½ cup prepared horseradish
4 pita bread rounds, cut into halves
1 onion, thinly sliced
4 romaine lettuce leaves
1 red bell pepper, cut lengthwise into ¼-inch-thick slices
1 green bell pepper, cut lengthwise into ¼-inch-thick slices

1. Preheat oven to 400°F. Place pork tenderloins in roasting pan; brush with barbecue sauce.

2. Bake tenderloins 15 minutes; turn and bake 15 minutes or until internal temperature reaches 155°F. Cover with foil; let stand 15 minutes.

3. Slice pork across grain. Spread horseradish on pita bread halves; stuff with pork, onion, lettuce and bell peppers. Garnish, if desired.
Makes 4 servings

Nutrients per Serving:

Calories: 440, Total Fat: 9 g, Cholesterol: 121 mg, Sodium: 628 mg

Fresh Rockfish Burger

ACKNOWLEDGMENTS

The publisher would like to thank the companies and organizations listed below for the use of their recipes and photographs in this publication.

A.1.® Steak Sauce

Alpine Lace Brands, Inc.

Birds Eye®

Bob Evans®

Dole Food Company, Inc.

EGG BEATERS® Healthy Real Egg Substitute

FLEISCHMANN'S® Original Spread

GREY POUPON® Mustard

Guiltless Gourmet®

The HV Company

The Kingsford Products Company

Kraft Foods, Inc.

Lawry's® Foods, Inc.

Lipton®

National Foods

National Pork Producers Council

National Turkey Federation

Nestlé USA, Inc.

Norseland, Inc.

North Dakota Beef Commission

Reckitt & Colman Inc.

Riviana Foods Inc.

Sargento® Foods Inc.

StarKist® Seafood Company

USA Rice Federation

Veg-All®

Walnut Marketing Board

Wisconsin Milk Marketing Board

INDEX

METRIC CONVERSION CHART

VOLUME MEASUREMENTS (dry)

$\frac{1}{8}$ teaspoon = 0.5 mL
$\frac{1}{4}$ teaspoon = 1 mL
$\frac{1}{2}$ teaspoon = 2 mL
$\frac{3}{4}$ teaspoon = 4 mL
1 teaspoon = 5 mL
1 tablespoon = 15 mL
2 tablespoons = 30 mL
$\frac{1}{4}$ cup = 60 mL
$\frac{1}{3}$ cup = 75 mL
$\frac{1}{2}$ cup = 125 mL
$\frac{2}{3}$ cup = 150 mL
$\frac{3}{4}$ cup = 175 mL
1 cup = 250 mL
2 cups = 1 pint = 500 mL
3 cups = 750 mL
4 cups = 1 quart = 1 L

VOLUME MEASUREMENTS (fluid)

1 fluid ounce (2 tablespoons) = 30 mL
4 fluid ounces ($\frac{1}{2}$ cup) = 125 mL
8 fluid ounces (1 cup) = 250 mL
12 fluid ounces (1$\frac{1}{2}$ cups) = 375 mL
16 fluid ounces (2 cups) = 500 mL

WEIGHTS (mass)

$\frac{1}{2}$ ounce = 15 g
1 ounce = 30 g
3 ounces = 90 g
4 ounces = 120 g
8 ounces = 225 g
10 ounces = 285 g
12 ounces = 360 g
16 ounces = 1 pound = 450 g

DIMENSIONS

$\frac{1}{16}$ inch = 2 mm
$\frac{1}{8}$ inch = 3 mm
$\frac{1}{4}$ inch = 6 mm
$\frac{1}{2}$ inch = 1.5 cm
$\frac{3}{4}$ inch = 2 cm
1 inch = 2.5 cm

OVEN TEMPERATURES

250°F = 120°C
275°F = 140°C
300°F = 150°C
325°F = 160°C
350°F = 180°C
375°F = 190°C
400°F = 200°C
425°F = 220°C
450°F = 230°C

BAKING PAN SIZES

Utensil	Size in Inches/Quarts	Metric Volume	Size in Centimeters
Baking or	8×8×2	2 L	20×20×5
Cake Pan	9×9×2	2.5 L	23×23×5
(square or	12×8×2	3 L	30×20×5
rectangular)	13×9×2	3.5 L	33×23×5
Loaf Pan	8×4×3	1.5 L	20×10×7
	9×5×3	2 L	23×13×7
Round Layer	8×1½	1.2 L	20×4
Cake Pan	9×1½	1.5 L	23×4
Pie Plate	8×1¼	750 mL	20×3
	9×1¼	1 L	23×3
Baking Dish	1 quart	1 L	—
or Casserole	1½ quart	1.5 L	—
	2 quart	2 L	—